A WORLD GONE BY

Lightmoor Press

Lightmoor Press is an imprint of
Black Dwarf Lightmoor Publications Limited
144b Lydney Industrial Estate, Harbour Road
Lydney, Gloucestershire, GL15 4EJ
Printed and bound by Berforts Information Press, Eynsham, Oxfordshire

A WORLD GONE BY
Recollections of Ernest Bartlett Taylor

Wimbledon to Witney
Electrical Engineer to Builder

The gateway in High Street, Witney, leading into the builder's yard of Bartlett Brothers.

edited and compiled by
Rosemary Warner and Dr Jane Cavell

ACKNOWLEDGEMENTS

Witney & District Museum for their hospitality
Stanley Jenkins for some timely introductions
Jimmy Dingle for sharing his knowledge of Bartlett Brothers
Richard Fisher for sharing his knowledge of building techniques
Professor Mick Aston for his permission to use illustrations from his book *Stonesfield Slates*
King's College School, Wimbledon for permission to use the plan of the school
Diana Smith for transcribing some of the early sections of the text
Toni Pull for the photograph of Jack Bartlett in RAF uniform
Kate Bradley for the photograph of Sandford Mount, Charlbury
June and Paul Smith for checking the text and for their suggestions
Richard Bartlett for his support and for unearthing many family artefacts
Donald Warner for his tolerance whilst Rosemary buried room after room in paperwork
Jane Cavell would like to thank her family and friends for their patience and is sorry for neglecting them

A glimpse of part of the stores in the yard of Bartlett Builders.

CONTENTS

An accident at the Buttercross, Witney in March 1899.

PREFACE

The following pages tell the story of Ernest Bartlett Taylor, who was known to his family and close friends as Barry. It is a story that could easily have been relegated to a number of cardboard boxes had it not been for some chance meetings and the renewal of an old acquaintance.

After his retirement Barry, who was my father's cousin, presented me, from time to time, with pieces of densely typed text (he didn't do paragraphs), boxes of photographs and bundles of family letters. All he would say was *"Would you like these?"* I was fascinated to receive this wealth of material. He gave no indication as to what should be done with it all but I supposed, at length, that he must have regarded me as a caretaker.

When Barry died in October 1990 he left all his remaining papers and documents to my brother, Richard Bartlett, and myself with the instruction *"to dispose of as they think most appropriate with the request that nothing shall be destroyed hastily"*. The vast quantity of material could only be processed over a long period of time. Many items have now been presented to the Witney & District Museum, where some have already been professionally conserved. Over the years the painstaking process of transcribing the documents, not an easy task, made the idea of publishing any of the material too daunting.

In 2009, I renewed my acquaintance with the Reverend John Cook who had been a close friend of Barry. I shared some of the text with him and together we journeyed through the pages, sharing anecdotes and building a clearer picture of what could be achieved if the writings were assembled together. Gradually, because of his enthusiasm, I reached the point where I had the motivation and confidence to make a start on the project.

In 2011, I was fortunate to meet Stanley Jenkins, who also had known Barry and who had received from Barry information about the Bartlett family and the beginnings of the building firm. Stanley, as part of his support for Witney & District Museum, had been involved with the conservation of some of the Bartlett ledgers that Richard and I had donated some years previously. I was delighted to see the results. I was also delighted to be introduced to Dr Jane Cavell, a genealogist, with a keen interest in and knowledge of the history of Witney. Jane and I joined forces to see if it would be possible to sort the parts of Barry's story into a publication of general interest.

Witney & District Museum provided us with a meeting place and an area where we could work on the text and the accompanying photographs. The rooms where we worked were in the same building complex in which a major part of the story had unfolded

Malachi Bartlett

and it is likely that Barry wrote most of his memoirs in these same buildings. Together, Jane and I were able to move the project forward, from what could have been just an interesting idea, on to something more tangible. Jane brought a new eye to the project – whereas I was familiar with many of the characters we encountered, she was able to question connections and apply her expertise to elements of the family tree. We have retained as far as possible Barry's own style, for example, he tended to use surnames as a means of address; this can sometimes appear quite stark.

Unless otherwise stated, all the illustrations come from our family collection; many of the pictures were taken by Barry himself and a good few by his close relatives although it is only possible to make a guess at who these individuals might have been – the ones missing from family groups perhaps? In places within the story, Barry seems to have an inordinate number of cousins. He had eight first cousins but his grandmother, Jessie Bartlett (née Knock), had four sisters and six brothers many of whom had children and there was a great deal of interaction between these families. Barry's escapades with his friends in London can easily be followed in a modern A-Z map of London, however, the environment he describes differs considerably from the one experienced today.

Much of the original material is in draft form. Barry had divided it into four major parts but some sections from other of his writings have been introduced into the main text to build on the atmosphere of some of his recollections. We have changed few of his words and have checked facts as far as possible, but we were not able to trace a few individuals, some of whom Barry knew as a small child. We have subdivided each of the main parts of his story, using his own words to make headings in the text.

We have for the time being only covered the span of Barry's life; there is much more material of social and historical interest that has to be analysed. Malachi Bartlett, Barry's great-grandfather on his mother's side, founded his building firm, in Witney, in the nineteenth century. Many of the records of Malachi's story together with his family's letters, will form the basis of a further publication which is currently in preparation. Although Barry does not mention Malachi in *A World Gone By*, I am confident that he would approve of his inclusion here.

Rosemary Warner
Witney
2012

The family of Ernest Bartlett Taylor (Barry). At the centre are his grandparents, Joseph Malachi Bartlett with his wife Jessie (née Knock). Pictured to the left is Caroline, Barry's mother, and from the rear, left to right, his uncles Oswald, Ernest, Joseph Francis, Percy and Christopher.

PROLOGUE

It is one of the inevitable hardships and privileges of advancing years that one tends to look more and more at the past, if not through a glass darkly, through glasses that are likely to be rose coloured. Now with my three score years and ten well behind me, I can look back on the conditions that have prevailed in my small world over the past seventy years and gather together the impressions that are left with the nostalgia that persists. I look back on a world that is very real to me with feelings of pleasure and however improbably coloured that picture may be, it does no harm to contemplate.

By chance or good fortune, I have known those who belonged to a generation that saw the end of ways that went back over a thousand years – ways that have changed so much, even in my lifetime, that few can now remember what life was like before the advent of all the technology that has become so much part of our lives.

My thoughts and impressions are not necessarily right or wrong, good or bad but I hope that in setting down what I can still remember (however crudely) this may provide a general picture that may be of interest; I feel that it is better to include minor details of things and happenings that are of little importance in themselves but which nevertheless may give colour and atmosphere to the whole.

I hope to provide some sort of picture of both the impressions and the feelings that I have experienced during my own life; I know that any such record of the lives of my parents or grandparents would have delighted me had one been available in some form or other. With this in mind, I hope that whatever I write will prove of some interest to someone and I would ask you to bear in mind that it is a frank expression of my thoughts written not, I hope, with any egotistical or self righteous motive but in an endeavour to provide some insights into a way of life and happenings of the immediate past.

Part One
EARLY YEARS, WIMBLEDON & WITNEY

Five hundred salmon parr and a birth

In 1900 Thames Ditton was little more than a village; it was situated to the south of a bend in the river Thames and to the north, across the river, lay Hampton Court and beyond this Bushey Park. To the west was Imber Court Park and to the south was open country as far as Oxshott. The surroundings were quite rural and, in those days, the suburban sprawl which was so soon to appear, had hardly reached as far as Kingston which was a convenient shopping centre and lay a mile or so to the east. Behind the waterfront and the church were a few shops and to the south, adjoining the main Portsmouth Road, was an extensive Green much used for cricket. Between the shops and a lane called Church Walk was a recently made road terminating at right angles to Church Walk. Here had been built a few small houses facing north towards the church and the river and in one of these my parents came to live in 1900.

Try to picture a world without noise or fumes, without motor cars or aeroplanes, without wireless or television and where a telephone was unusual. A world where there was little haste, where life could be savoured and enjoyed and where the countryside and rivers were unpolluted. On the 23rd April 1901 the Thames Salmon Association released five hundred salmon parr into the Thames just below Thames Ditton and this event was of more interest to the local inhabitants of Thames Ditton than my birth which occurred on the same day.

My early horizon was bounded by a slatted fence giving glimpses of a larger world and other children as I rested in the shade of a large greengage tree in the garden. Later I was wheeled in a bentwood push chair along the roads and paths, few of which were paved, to the shops, the church, the station and frequently to the river.

William Ernest Charles Taylor.
Born April 11th 1867, married February 27th 1900.

**Caroline Amelia Jessie Margaret Taylor, née Bartlett.
Born Dec 2nd 1863.**

Barry aged 2½ years with his mother Caroline – Carrie.

The floating landing stage was very much part of the village life and here were boats of all descriptions. Across the river lay Hampton Court with easy access by ferry and on the river I floated in a skiff or punt propelled by my father. Other transport was provided by a horse drawn bus that ran along the Portsmouth Road to Kingston and this stopped to pick up passengers at the Green; both this bus and the trains from the station were frequent and were within easy walking distance from where we lived.

Most of my impressions at this time are naturally somewhat dim but I have quite clear pictures of parts of the house: there was the long sitting room with doors opening to the garden through which I was led to pick nasturtium leaves to eat between bread and butter. The rather dark kitchen was where the maid fed me with a boiled egg and the hall and stairs were where I found myself alone and frightened because I could find no one in the house. I remember a barrel organ playing in the road and being taken to see the monkey on it and a large red motor car with a sloping bonnet (my Uncle Oswald had arrived from Brook Green). Tables were laid with glass and silver gleaming on white cloths and lit by candles and oil lamps. All these impressions must have been very early ones and I cannot recall much of the remainder of the interior of the house such as bedrooms or a bathroom.

Along the road towards Church Walk stood a house occupied by the Harts who were friends of my parents; this was a larger house pleasantly situated in a large garden and I have many clear memories of playing there with their daughter, Eileen, who was about my age. This house had been a wedding present from

Barry aged 2½ years.

Mrs Hart's parents who owned extensive market gardens west of Isleworth; here large areas were cultivated and the produce sent to Covent Garden Market. I was told that the area was irrigated by water drawn by hand from shallow wells by means of a long pole hinged to a post. I remember their house and its surroundings very clearly probably because I visited it again after we had left Thames Ditton. All my impressions are of a sunlit world where everything moved slowly and horses and people did not hurry. This was a golden age when people had time to 'sit and drink, sit and think or just sit'.

No doubt my first visit to the church was when I was christened but I was later taken to a wedding service which I remember quite well and this was probably intended as part of my education.

There were visits to Wimbledon where a new house was being built and on one of these I was taken to a shop in Durham Road and presented with a banana by my grandfather who had come to inspect the new house; this impressed me as something new but the picture of the house is only a dim one of an untidy mass of red bricks and heaps of soil.

My only memory of the move was my inspection of a large green pantechnicon drawn by horses and I watched furniture being packed into the interior which seemed large and dark and forbidding. My fourth birthday, the first I can remember, was celebrated in the new house at Wimbledon and I was presented with a small garden spade. On the following one, my fifth, I was given a small fork. If these offerings were intended to encourage any liking for gardening that I may have shown, they failed completely.

Although I was pleased with the tools at the time, further efforts to interest me in any form of work in the garden were wasted. I was given a small piece of garden, plants to put in, seeds to sow, sprouted potatoes to bury all to no purpose and later on, any grass cutting, sweeping up of leaves (of which there were a great many) or any form of work in the garden was something to be avoided.

The house fronted onto a newly made road which soon ran out and became a completely wild grass-grown lane; this was my playground and I spent what seemed endless summer days here bird nesting, catching frogs, butterflies and moths, playing by myself and exploring what was a new world that included a thatched cottage where lots of goats were tethered. I did not stray very far from this lane but on one occasion I was found by my father in a field near Walpole Road where I had joined forces with some local boys who were helping (?) to erect a roundabout on which we hoped for a free ride. I was sent home.

The garden at the side of the house had a long frontage to Durham Road and here were several large elm trees and a few oaks; these provided the opportunity for a lot of climbing practice and also enabled me to drop stones and other objects onto passing vehicles and pedestrians using the road below. In the roots of these trees and in the oak posts of the adjoining fence were found large white grubs which I discovered later became stag beetles with large horns; these and other features of the garden provided lots of interest. There was a swing and a hammock in the garden. From the former I fell out from quite a height and still bear the scars. In the latter I had an ambition to sleep the night but always returned to the house before morning.

At Elmside, Oswald, Maud and Jack Bartlett (grouped left) with Barry and his parents, Ernest and Caroline together with Edith Kate – Kitty, Bartlett (née Hughes).

Later there was cricket practice on the lawn when I could persuade my father to bowl for me. While playing here one evening I heard an unfamiliar sound and, looking up, saw an object in the sky travelling slowly from east to west. This was the first aircraft I had seen and I learned later that it was piloted by Graham White. It was a pusher type biplane and I could see, quite clearly, the pilot wearing goggles sitting in front quite unprotected. It was about this time that a Frenchman, living in a house a few hundred yards down the hill, was busy constructing an aeroplane in his garden and we spent many hours watching this. It was made of wood and metal tubes and was powered by a motor cycle from which the wheels had been removed. This drove cranks that imparted an up and down motion to the wings and also drove a propeller. I heard later that he took it onto the Common for tests but it is unlikely that it ever flew.

Here on this Common we watched man-lifting kites, held by a winch, being flown; the unfortunate passenger was contained in a small wicker basket. Here also we spent many hours flying our own kites, which were quite large, and once, when I was with Herbert and Bessie Ward, theirs came adrift and was lost over the south side and never seen gain.

The Wards were neighbours and friends of my parents and I spent a lot of time with the two children who were a few years older than I was; I was particularly attracted by a small workshop they had in the garden and by a photographic dark room in the house. I watched with great interest the construction of an internal combustion engine. Wooden patterns were made, castings machined on a small treadle lathe and a complete horizontal engine resulted which actually worked. The Wards were extremely kind and long suffering and took me on numerous expeditions

with them – on the river at Kingston, swimming at the baths and once on a holiday at Leysdown in the Isle of Sheppey.

From a very early age I could swim quite well and before I was seven I was diving from the top board. My father took me to the steam baths in the City, early morning bathing in the Queensmere on the Common and to Brighton where I dived off the pier.

Transport was easy; there were horse buses at the bottom of Durham Road (and later trams) and a local railway station, with another at Wimbledon; London was only about twenty minutes away. Horse cabs were not often used and my father taught me to ride on my mother's cycle before I could reach the pedals from the saddle. Otherwise walking was accepted as the normal way to get about and we covered considerable distances without concern.

The house, Elmside, was situated at the junction of Durham Road with Cottenham Park Road with extensive views to the south over Cheam and Ewell as far as Epsom racecourse. To the north lay the Common about half a mile away and at the bottom of Durham Road, along Worple Road about a mile, was Wimbledon town. Raynes Park had developed around the railway station and a few groups of shops were situated lower down Durham Road between Elmside and Raynes Park. There were a number of fair sized houses built in the nineteenth century in Cottenham Park Road lying to the east but the rest of this road was of recent development; the western portion was still the original old lane, quite wild and undeveloped.

There were a several of these tracks and unmade lanes in the area which must have been part of the original estate; thatched cottages and groups of buildings, roofed with local red tiles, abounded although a lot of development had taken place around the Common and Wimbledon and Raynes Park areas.

Elmside, Cottenham Park Road, Wimbledon.

From the lower, Raynes Park, end of Durham Road was a gradual rise which increased to a steep hill outside Elmside and this hill continued round the bend into Cottenham Park Road where it remained steep almost as far as the junction with the Ridgeway. It was a difficult climb for horses and a water trough was provided at the top. On the right, the Ridgeway continued as far as the top of the main hill out of Wimbledon to the Common and on this hill a trace horse was always available to help with the loads.

Turning left from Cottenham Park Road, the Ridgeway became Copse Hill which descended in a long curve to meet the main Kingston Road through Coombe Lane. Here were extensive woods, full of bluebells in the spring and a notice 'Beware of Man Traps'. The Common was approached from Cottenham Park Road via Woodhays Road and, on the right and facing the Common, was King's College School. Over the Common was first the Rushmere Pond, further on the Windmill and beyond this Kingsmere Lake. Lower down and to the west was Queensmere and beyond this to the north-west lay Richmond Park. South of the Windmill were the old butts which had been opened in July 1860 for rifle firing and it was here that my grandfather, Joseph Bartlett, won many prizes. Only the main roads were tarred and the others, formed of gravel, were always covered in flints; these played havoc with rubber tyres and shoe leather and a number of footpaths were also finished in gravel. The Common was crossed by many tracks and there were lots of unmade roads and lanes.

When I first attended the school in Worple Road (about 1909) this was approached through grass-grown lanes. The swimming baths were situated on the east side of Wimbledon, about two miles from Elmside, in Latimer Road and to get there it was necessary to go right through Wimbledon town which, even in those days, was quite busy.

I have no recollection of boredom although little or no money was spent on amusement, there was no television or wireless and visits to the cinema were very infrequent. The nearest cinema was about a mile along Worple Road and was managed by a man named Huddleston who later came to Witney. I had friends in the Wards, Webbs and Howells and we made our own amusements and never seemed to lack plenty to do. We carried boats to sail on the ponds on the Common, flew kites and travelled long distances on foot; a red letter day was when all the traffic, open carriages and horses, came past the house on Derby Day and the Oaks.

I spent a lot of time trying to make things – boats, model aeroplanes etc. – and later I installed a bench in my bedroom. Looking back, I am amazed how long suffering my mother was with the mess I made with wood, glue and metal in this room. Money was never easy to get and when I needed elastic strands to propel models, there was not enough to buy this and pay a bus fare so I had to walk to the shop with my penny or twopence. Wood for a boat cost fourpence and had to be saved over two weeks. Later I used the cupboard under the stairs as a dark room and from here I obtained access to the area under the ground floor of the house. This made an excellent shooting range and, having first acquired a 'Daisy' air gun from someone at Witney, my father bought me a .22 rifle which cost, new, the sum of 12/6 (unbelievable!). This was quite lethal and I was stopped from using it in the garden, but under the floors I got in a lot of target practice when I could afford the ammunition. I had a habit of loading from a supply held in my mouth until I swallowed a cartridge. This appeared to do me no harm but necessitated a dose of castor oil. Later still, I acquired

quite an armoury of rifles and pistols (some with sawn-off barrels) and I mixed quite effective gunpowder for use in a home-made cannon; other explosive was obtained by opening cartridges and extracting the cordite, all of which was more than dangerous.

We seldom wore shoes

Two summer holidays remain outstanding in my mind, the first was a visit to my mother's Uncle Alfred and Aunt Isobel who lived in a cottage at Hope Cove in Devon; this must have taken place about 1906/7. The house was quite near the harbour and my father and I sometimes walked down before breakfast and were taken out by a fisherman into the bay where we caught fish to cook for breakfast. I was thrilled to sail with a following wind, at what seemed to me, greater speeds than I had ever travelled.

At the end of their garden, over a wall and across a small field was a path down the cliff which led to a beach that was quite private. Here we frequently bathed, entirely alone and undisturbed. In some of the caves we found large pieces of pure rubber which I was told had been washed up from a wreck on the rocks at Bolt Tail. This was my first introduction to the sea. I was impressed by all the smells of seaweed and fish and the rocks and caves that abounded; we experienced complete freedom from haste or anything artificial.

After the long train journey, the drive from Kingsbridge in a horse-drawn brake, with everything of interest pointed out to me, together with the profusion of colours and unfamiliar smells, made

Alfred Knock, Carrie's uncle.

13

a lasting impression on me; I am sure that my parents enjoyed it and there seemed nothing to mar this enjoyment at that time. My father remarked afterwards that he had been ashamed of his appetite. It was the one and only time I ever saw my mother bathing, dressed in a voluminous dark serge costume reaching to her ankles. She almost learned to swim.

The second holiday was spent with the Wards at Leysdown on the Isle of Sheppey. This must have been about 1911. We went by train and walked from the station across the fields to the house at Leysdown, one of a small group that took in paying guests. There were no shops and few roads. We seldom wore shoes and I remember the feel of grass and grit on bare feet.

The country was flat and open with few buildings. Sheerness was about seven or eight miles away and I remember walking past the dockyard to get there. Some nearer shops were at Eastchurch and Minster, about two and five miles respectively. The coast at Leysdown provided safe and easy bathing. We rowed in the bay and enjoyed the sight of the red sailed barges and the red cliffs at Warden Point. We fished for eels at low tide and carried them home, still alive, to be cooked and eaten. All our journeys seemed by way of grass tracks and lanes. When I met my father coming to see me, on the walk from the station, he took me into a farm and bought me a glass of milk.

Here on the beach near Eastchurch I saw my first seaplane; this was a biplane fitted with large floats and was being pulled onto the beach by several men who were being told what to do by a man with an enormous head. His name, I was told, was Short. My informant added that he, Short, was believed to have sold his head for examination after his death, but I have never heard this confirmed. The walk to Eastchurch or Minster, for some small purchase, was treated very lightly and I well remember a visit to Sheerness. As I can remember no form of transport, I imagine we must have walked but the distance, there and back, must have exceeded fifteen miles. All my memories of the Wards are pleasant ones. Although I had a great deal of freedom, I think they had a good influence on me and I shall always be grateful to them for the trouble they took to look after what must have been a responsibility and a nuisance to them.

Most other holidays were spent with my grandparents at Witney which I looked on as a second home. In fact, my mother and I spent long periods here when my father was away on business, particularly in the winters.

Tame mice in my desk

My first experience of school was in Witney, when I was sent to Miss Tarrant's school on the east side of Church Green in the winter of 1904/5. I could not have been there very long although I may have returned again the following winter, but I have very clear and complete pictures of all that I learned and all that I saw.

The side entrance led down a passage to the playground, a small area in the angle of the main building, and beyond this was an area of garden bordered by low box hedges, on the right was a square building, disused I think and covered in ivy, and on the left was the earth closet behind the main house. A door from the playground led into the house and on the left down a passage was the main front door; this was always used to go home but seldom on arrival,

Miss Tarrant, Carrie and Mrs Tarrant with Barry's cousins Jessie and Dorrie Bartlett – in the Bartlett's Close at Witney.

on the right was the staircase and at the foot of this the door to a large kitchen where Miss Tarrant reigned. I do not remember that she ever taught but she was always available in this kitchen and I was once taken there, seated on the table, and made to promise not to repeat some misdemeanour although I still have no idea what this was. I liked her as I did Miss Bird and Miss Fairburn who both taught me in the classrooms above. I think I could already read in some way but we practised copperplate writing and were taught how to start and finish a letter written to our parents, also much scripture, arithmetic and spelling. In the short time I was there I learned a great deal that has remained with me. I look on this early period as a most important part of such education that I had.

I still remember many of the pupils that were there with me – many more than at any other school – and particularly the Walkers, Will and Guy, the Mawles, Ted and Cyril, Ted Holtom and, quite clearly, those who accompanied me when we walked home, Elsie and Dorothy Felton and Kitty, Janie and Ena List; probably they had been asked to see me safely home on their own journey to Northfield Farm (quite a long walk, four times a day). Some came from still further away on foot, by horse and trap and by train of which there were at least five to and from Witney each day.

One outstanding event was the Christmas party with tables in the classrooms and jellies, iced cake, crackers and games which were all a great treat to us. This memory has remained as a very clear picture as has also the arrival of Ted and Cyril Mawle on a donkey, of being led to the earth closet in the garden by lantern light and being told to say 'thank you' before going home.

Most schools at this time were provided with slates in a wood frame written on with a small round slate pencil which usually squeaked. Each pupil owned a pencil box cut from solid wood; it had a sliding top which uncovered a grooved receptacle for pencils and an eraser and this could be swung to one side to reveal another receptacle below. Some exercise books and a blackboard were provided but textbooks were few.

My recollections of whatever education I had immediately following my attendance at Miss Tarrant's school are extremely dim. My mother taught me a great deal of basic knowledge and until the spring of 1910, I cannot remember any other school. When I was nine I was sent to a school in Worple Road called The Ruskin School kept by a Miss Stewart, here I can remember very little of the actual school, none of the pupils and still less of what I was taught. My main impression is of a red bag in which shoes were deposited on arrival. The journey to and fro of about a mile was by way of lanes in which were a profusion of dog roses and I was accompanied by two small girls whose names were Gwynneth and Rhowna Webb. They lived in a house below Elmside and I was told that they were connected in some way with the Masons family and went to stay at Eynsham Hall near Witney.

The continuity of my education was obviously affected by the periods spent at Witney during the winters and while this was unsettling, it certainly gave me a wide variety of experience of schools. The next that I attended was 'Rokeby', a preparatory school of some standing situated in the Downs, midway between the Ridgeway and Worple Road and where, during the summer of 1911, I spent much time learning to dress properly and to play cricket. The standard of education was probably very good but it left little impression on my memory and I attended for only one term.

Barry's report from Ruskin School, Wimbledon 1910.

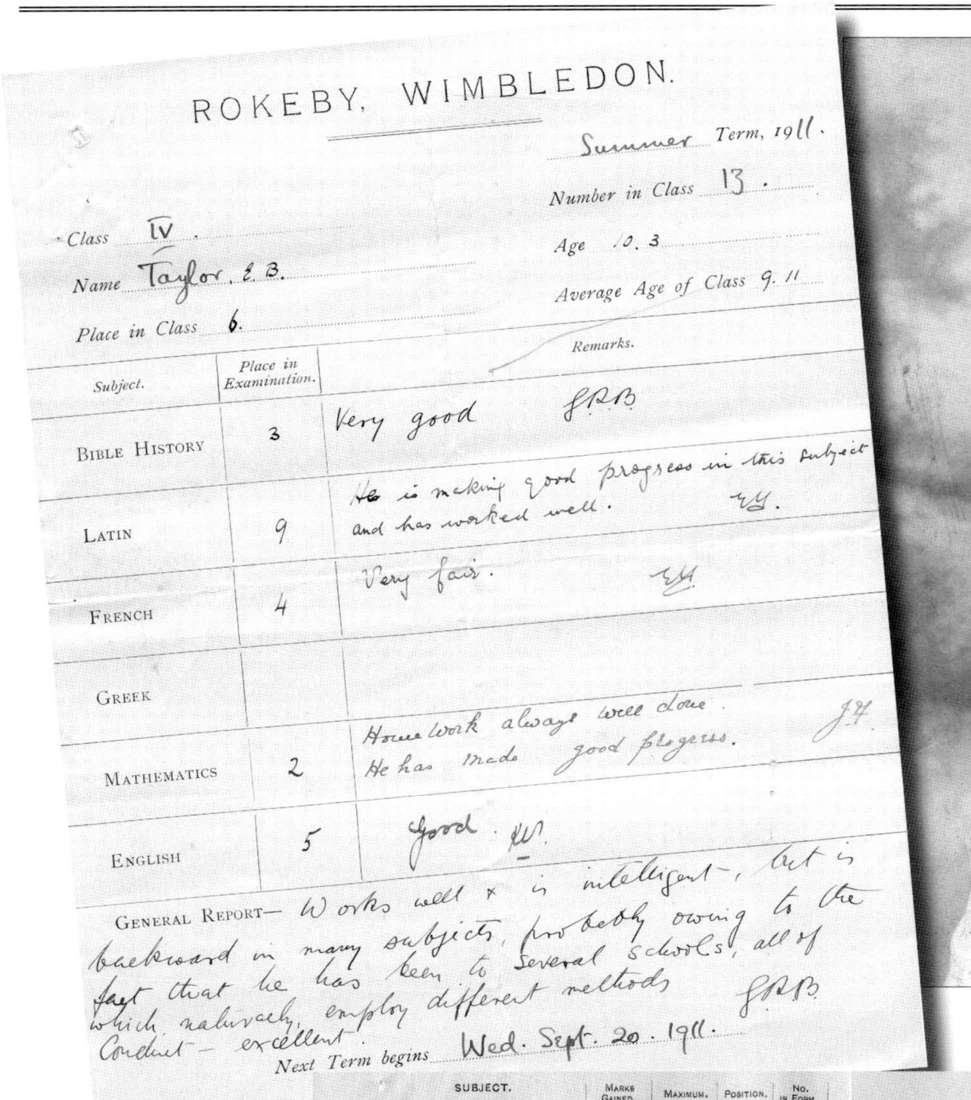

ROKEBY, WIMBLEDON.

Summer Term, 1911.

Number in Class 13.

Class IV.

Name Taylor, E. B.

Age 10.3

Average Age of Class 9.11

Place in Class 6.

Subject.	Place in Examination.	Remarks.
BIBLE HISTORY	3	Very good G.R.B
LATIN	9	He is making good progress in this subject and has worked well. E.H.
FRENCH	4	Very fair. E.H.
GREEK		
MATHEMATICS	2	Home work always well done. J.T. He has made good progress.
ENGLISH	5	Good. H.P.

GENERAL REPORT— Works well & is intelligent, but is backward in many subjects, probably owing to the fact that he has been to several schools, all of which naturally, employ different methods G.R.B.
Conduct — excellent.

Next Term begins Wed. Sept. 20. 1911.

Above: A report from Rokeby School, Wimbledon. Note the comment concerning the fact that he had attended several schools.

Right: Barry's marks at Ruskin School.

Barry at Rokeby School.

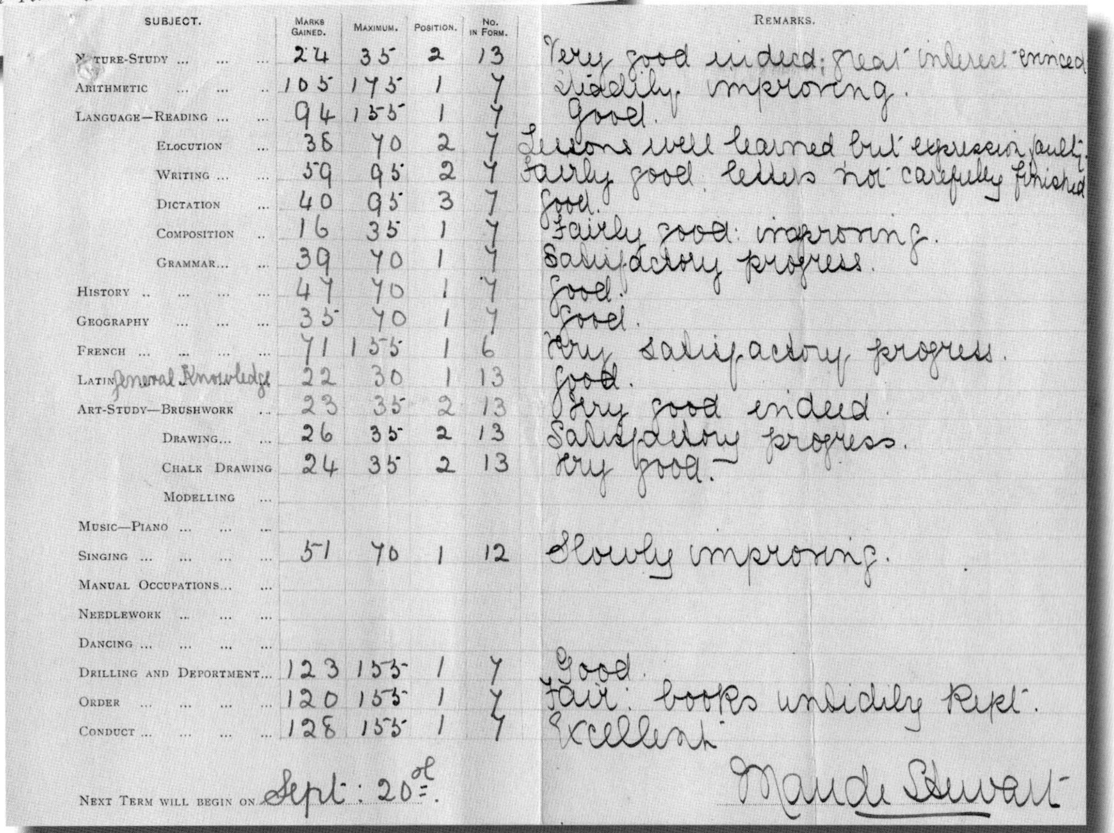

SUBJECT.	MARKS GAINED.	MAXIMUM.	POSITION.	NO. IN FORM.	REMARKS.
NATURE-STUDY	24	35	2	13	Very good indeed; great interest evinced.
ARITHMETIC	105	175	1	7	Steadily improving.
LANGUAGE—READING	94	155	1	7	Good.
ELOCUTION	38	70	2	7	Lessons well learned but expression faulty
WRITING	59	95	2	7	Fairly good. letters not carefully finished
DICTATION	40	95	3	7	Good.
COMPOSITION	16	35	1	7	Fairly good. improving.
GRAMMAR	39	70	1	7	Satisfactory progress.
HISTORY	47	70	1	7	Good.
GEOGRAPHY	35	70	1	7	Good.
FRENCH	71	155	1	6	Very satisfactory progress.
LATIN General Knowledge	22	30	1	13	Good.
ART-STUDY—BRUSHWORK	23	35	2	13	Very good indeed.
DRAWING	26	35	2	13	Satisfactory progress.
CHALK DRAWING	24	35	2	13	Very good.—
MODELLING					
MUSIC—PIANO					
SINGING	51	70	1	12	Slowly improving.
MANUAL OCCUPATIONS					
NEEDLEWORK					
DANCING					
DRILLING AND DEPORTMENT	123	155	1	7	Good.
ORDER	120	155	1	7	Fair. books untidily kept.
CONDUCT	128	155	1	7	Excellent.

NEXT TERM WILL BEGIN ON Sept: 20=

Maude Stewart

The following summer I started at a school at the far end of the Ridgeway and to which I cycled each day about a mile and a half from Elmside. This was called Wimbledon Collegiate School and was run by a Mr Redman who managed to teach me quite a lot. It was well run, the discipline was good and we were made to work without being driven, in fact, I enjoyed being there as much as I enjoyed any school. I was always lazy, disliked having to make any effort to learn and resented any form of control, but I think Mr Redman got more out of me than any other school I went to.

We played cricket in a leisurely sort of way which I enjoyed; I liked the master, whose name I have forgotten, who played with us and this was probably because on occasions he took us to a local shop to drink lemonade. The impressions left with me of this period are: tame mice in my desk, these I had acquired from a boy (later I took them home and kept them in a cage in the cycle shed) …. a fight with a boy named Andrews, in which I acquired a black eye and other damage …. being reprimanded for cutting games one afternoon …. wearing long trousers for the first time.

I left this school in the autumn and went back to Witney, however I was sent back to the Collegiate School the following spring and remained there as far as I can remember until I went to King's College School early in 1914, where I remained until my father died in 1917.

In addition to these schools at Wimbledon, all of which I attended for very short periods, I had a short session at the Misses Walkers' school, Hillside, in Witney as well as Miss Tarrant's. For a brief period I attended the Witney Grammar School which I disliked; I learned very little and it had a bad influence on me. The demeanour of Haines, the headmaster, frightened me and the general atmosphere was poor. Fees were about £3 a term. I went to a total of six different schools before going to King's College School when I was twelve years old. Here I had the continuity that was so lacking in the preceding period and I was given the opportunity of a good sound public school education – if I was prepared to avail myself of it.

Right: **Barry's report from Wimbledon Collegiate School.**

Barry in 1912 - wearing long trousers!

WIMBLEDON COLLEGIATE SCHOOL

HEADMASTER'S REPORT

on *Ernest B. Taylor* aged *11* years *3* months

in Form *III* for the Term ending *July 27* 1912

SUBJECT	WORK OF TERM	MARKS	OUT OF
Reading and Recitation	Very good	75	100
English Literature	Fair	30	"
Grammar	Very good.	80	"
Composition	Fairly good.	60	"
Dictation and Spelling	do	55	"
Writing	Good.	70	"
Scripture History	do	50	"
English History	do	70	"
Geography and Mapping	do	70	"
French (Oral)	Making rapid progress.	65	"
French (Written)	do	45	"
~~German, Latin, Shorthand~~	Fairly good.	45	"
Arithmetic	do	55	"
Algebra	–	–	"
Geometry	Making good progress.	35	"
Natural Science	do	55	"
Drawing	Good	75	"
Music	Fair	30	"
Gymnastics	Making good progress.	50	"
Total Marks		1015	

Attendance: Times Early *115* Times Late *0* Times Absent *0*

Conduct: Excellent — I have been much pleased with Barts steady & intelligent work. He ought to do exceedingly well. *Hy. F. Redman. BA* Head Master

Barry with his parents, 1914.

Amusements were self made

Previously my life was divided into what seemed to me two distinct compartments. At Wimbledon it followed a typical suburban middle class pattern, at school I mixed with the same class of boy, my associates were limited and selected. I took part in many of the social activities of my parents including even the 'at home days' which my mother held on certain Tuesdays, to a regular schedule, when acquaintances called with strict etiquette and were fed on thin rolled bread and butter in the drawing room.

We seemed to have frequent visitors who stayed for periods or who were entertained at musical evenings and whom we visited in turn at their own homes. Among them I remember the Potters who lived at Ilford and who owned a beautifully made, coach-built carriage used by their daughter and drawn by a goat (but I never saw the goat); I think they had a chemist's business in Ilford. Mr Stanbrook, I believe, was unmarried and played the violin very well, he was a vet but I have no knowledge of where he lived. Harry Noakes, who also played the violin, lived in Kensington and was one of three brothers who had shared a house with my father before he married; Harry travelled abroad extensively and sent me numerous pictures of where

Ernest Taylor and Arthur Potter.

he was staying. He maintained a friendship with me after my father died. Trevellion, my father's partner, came infrequently and Steer, his junior partner, quite frequently. Steer and his family lived in South London, at Streatham or Croydon, where we went to see them; he had married the daughter of a wealthy American and they had a son, Lito, who was a few years my junior. I never got on very well with him but I saw him in later years when he was at Oxford in the 1920s. When playing with him in the garden at Elmside, I showed him how to make sparks by striking flints with a hammer and was told that this was a possible source of danger to the eyes.

The Morses came frequently and as he was a member of the Zoological Society, we had frequent trips to the Zoo on Sundays; they had a flat at Chelsea with elaborate window boxes full of flowers. Other people who stayed were Miss Bateman, a cousin of my father, and Aunt Lydia, from Leicester. She had brought up my father at Peatling Farm. Usually she was accompanied by her nieces, Lizzie and Lily, who lived with her after she moved to Leicester and my father also often went to stay with them. My Uncle Joe and his wife Nancy stayed with us on one occasion. My grandfather stayed only once and my grandmother infrequently, whilst numerous other friends and relations came to stay on short visits.

Relatives on Barry's father's side of the family: Lydia (Lily) Howitt, Barry, Aunt Lydia Egglesdon and Lizzie.

My father played quite a lot of golf and occasionally some men's tennis. The golf clubhouse was on the Common. I remember the locker room, a long bar and a large number of caddies waiting outside. Adjoining the clubhouse was a concrete area which I was told was flooded in winter to provide a curling rink when there was sufficient frost. All the golfers playing on the Common wore a scarlet coat and red balls were used when there was snow or frost.

Although visits to concerts were probably infrequent I was taken to the Albert Hall, where I was very bored with the music and singing, but I enjoyed visits to the theatre and remember seeing Forbes Robertson in several plays and we frequently went to Gilbert & Sullivan operas in Wimbledon. Most amusements were self made and consisted of sailing boats on the ponds, flying kites, roller skating, wherever a smooth surface could be found, and riding on a home-made trolley. I spent a lot of time trying to make model boats, aeroplanes and other toys – all very crudely.

Tea on Sundays remains in my memory with a picture of my mother presiding over a long table set out with blue china and pouring from a large pot. There seemed a great many people in the house and garden. I remember the arrival of Uncle Oswald and his family in a large car which he parked in Cottenham Park

Above: **Joseph Francis Bartlett and his wife Nancy (née Clifford).**

Left: **Barry's grandmother, Jessie Bartlett.**

Ernest Taylor, Oswald and Jack Bartlett and Carrie.

Jack Hughes on his motorcycle.

Road, with Jack Hughes's motor cycle on the opposite verge …. someone taking apart another motor cycle on the east lawn …. Herbert Ward damaging a fence when he was allowed to try his hand at driving the car …. sitting on rugs on the south side of the house and playing with Jack Bartlett who tried to eat some camphor moth balls he had found in a drawer. This was a happy period and I am left with memories of those sunny days, pursuing butterflies and watching dragonflies in the sun …. the thrill of finding myself riding a bicycle unaided …. breakfast in the dining room with sun streaming through the east windows …. lying in a hammock or resting in the hot drawing room listening to the drone of a bluebottle …. growing red and white cacti in the greenhouse …. watching the sun set at the end of the lane and watching my mother sitting reading in the dusk at the window of my bedroom. All this was in complete contrast to the periods spent at Witney in the winters when my father was away during the main part of the week and when I saw little of him except at weekends; I looked forward to these very much.

Above: No's 71, 73 and 75 High Street, Witney prior to the building of the shop at No. 73.

Right: The gateway to the Yard at 75 High Street.

The Yard and workshops were my playground

I was never unhappy at Wimbledon, but life at Witney always attracted me and seemed more interesting probably because I almost ran wild in spite of sporadic efforts to send me to school. I mixed freely with local boys of my own age and spoke their language, I spent much time with the men working in the Yard and I went where and when I wished without, as far as my memory serves me, anyone questioning where I had been or what I was doing.

Prior to the building of the shop and flat in the gateway between No's 71 and 75 High Street, this covered area and the yard at the rear provided a familiar playground for me. The adjoining houses were then occupied by my grandfather and his brother Christopher. The yard was a convenient place not only for storage, but for their own personal use and it remained more or less as it had been before No. 75 and the yard were purchased. The stables and access to my grandfather's house were on the south side, with his office and coal store all opening into the covered area. On the north side was a grape vine, a long narrow office and access to No. 75. It was common ground for both houses. A car was kept there together with some traps and other vehicles including a bone-shaker bicycle.

Joseph Malachi Bartlett.

William Christopher Bartlett.

Horses were no longer kept in these stables but the harness and other equipment interested me and I played around the pump and horse trough. In the stables at the top end of the other yard there were still horses and I was a frequent visitor. In the winter it was warm and comfortable, lit by the stable lantern and I had the company of the carters, Busby and Forester (Thomas Keen), when the horses were being bedded down. I was lifted up to try to catch mice in the corn bin and sometimes was allowed to ride on Tommy to the water trough; I was told he was 17 hands high.

From my earliest childhood, I associated with workmen who were always kind and patient with me. I seemed to have almost complete freedom to wander at will without hindrance and there were many interests and distractions; the Yard and workshops were my playground. The blacksmith's shop was a particular favourite and I was never stopped from wandering about the generating station at the end of the yard; the engines and gas producers fascinated me. I made friends with all the men and at times must have been a great nuisance to them; I am surprised that few, if any, objected to my presence. I remember the plumber, Bill Townsend …. the blacksmith, Dore …. the joiners, Chris Harris and others …. the banker mason, John Rowles …. the slater, Jim Jordan …. the plasterer, Ellis Griffin …. the wheelwright, Charlie Richards …. Fred Busby, Forester, Jack Hall, Arthur Busby – all were my friends. I eagerly watched such operations as lime burning, horses being shod, beating hair, lathing, lining coffins, grinding paint, running lead cames and soldering lead lights. I climbed into lofts, under timber stacks and up ladders and came to no harm.

'Forester' –Thomas Keen – the origins of his nickname remain a mystery.

21

Above: **Uncles Joseph and Ernest with Barry c. 1905.**
Right: **Barry's rocking horse at Witney c. 1905.**

My grandfather had five sons and a daughter (my mother) and by 1903 all of them had married. I was his eldest grandchild and he gave me a lot of his attention. A great deal of the time that I spent in Witney was in his company; even at an early age some of the wisdom of his experience must have impressed itself on me because I remember so many details of what he told me and where we went. For example, when we watched steel joists being hoisted and set over Viner's shop front at 64 High Street, he told me what pad stones were for …. when he brought a mason to Wimbledon to set a range, he explained how flues worked …. when visiting the ironmonger, he showed me how glass was cut …. when we watched the tiled floor being laid in the hall of No. 79, before his son Percy went to live there, he explained why it was cleaned off with sawdust. When one was close by, I always ran to see a 'Puffing Billy' which was my grandfather's name for a steam traction engine.

My grandfather frequently took me with him when we walked to sites near home and sometimes we rode in the Benz car; this car is now part of the collection of the Science Museum. I recall the clouds of white dust that always seemed to accompany us on our journeys. We never went far away; we visited the quarry where I watched men working and breaking out what appeared to be vast lumps of golden stone using heavy quarry bars. We visited the brewery in the rain and viewed the black smouldering timbers after a fire. I saw the walls of the new blanket factory being built for Earlys after the disastrous fire that destroyed almost all of the old mill. I was interested in the engine that was driving the large mortar mill on the site of the stone cottages being built for Chubbs in Mill Lane and I remember seeing the old cottages being pulled down. When we were stranded, after the Benz stalled in a water splash, I was told that I had helped to get it going again. Another car I can remember is a single-cylinder Wolseley from which I parted company when rounding a corner at Ducklington. I was

A Benz car BW 37 used by Joseph Malachi around 1903/4. It was kept in the open gateway at 73 High Street where later the shop was built. Barry was allowed to sit in it and play with the controls. It is now owned by the Science Museum and is currently (2012) on exhibition at the National Motor Museum at Beaulieu.

A single-cylinder Wolseley used by Joseph M. about 1906.

unhurt but rather frightened – although probably less frightened than my grandfather; I have a clear memory of being comforted on a sofa at the Vicarage close by.

I was never lonely. My grandparents were very kind to me and I had five uncles and aunts and eight cousins who all visited the house frequently and we were always busy. In 1907 a shop and flat were built between No's 71 and 75 High Street, where the old gateway had formed the entrance to the Yard and the old disused stables were later divided off and included in the tenancy of the new shop.

Family group taken on October 6th 1906 – with several more children expected! Back row pictured from left to right: Percy Bartlett with Dorothy (Dorrie), Christopher Bartlett with Phyllis, Joseph M. Bartlett, Joseph F. M. Bartlett, Oswald Bartlett with Jack, Ernest Taylor and Ernest Bartlett. Front row, left to right: Beauty the greyhound, Barry, Blanche Bartlett (née Symonds) with Jessie, Jessie Bartlett (née Knock), Lettie Bartlett with Denis, Nancy Bartlett (née Clifford), Maud Bartlett, Carrie Taylor and Kitty Bartlett (née Hughes).

Barley Park c. 1914. Left to right: Denis, Bernard and Phyllis with Christopher and Violetta (Lettie) Bartlett née Jackson.

We were brought up with guns and rifles

At Witney, wherever we went my companions and I walked. I have previously mentioned the long distances travelled on foot and if I had a cycle at this time I made little use of it. Although Witney ranked as a town, it was mainly contained in two streets and behind these and all around was open country. The lane at the rear of the Closes was quite rural and from here, across the Moors, we journeyed via Dark Lane to the quarry where we spent many happy hours. There was the rock face to be climbed, rabbits to be snared, sheds to play in and opportunity to indulge in all the activities that children then enjoyed, including the forbidden one of smoking; this was probably infrequent but I remember that Nell Gwyn cigarettes of assorted flavours cost twopence halfpenny for ten, Players and Gold Flake threepence and Woodbines were five for penny – tobacco was about fourpence an ounce. Most of the names of the boys who accompanied me have vanished from my mind but I clearly remember Herbert Humphreys who lived in a cottage on Narrow Hill, Henry Wilsdon whose father farmed Park Farm, Max and Reggie Phillips who lived at Hillrise, whose father was a wine and spirit merchant and whose mother always made us welcome in the house, Ronald Ravenor and Sam Smith whose sister, Ann, was courted in the garden of The Gables by Oswald Tarrant.

There were frequent visits to Park Farm, reached by passing the quarry and proceeding up the lane at the side of the cemetery. Here there was a pony to ride and many other interests at the farm in the buildings and fields but it was the quarry that was our headquarters. It had all that we valued – privacy, empty buildings and sheds, trees and wild bushes, the quarry itself with piles of stones, rabbits and other wild life. No one disturbed us or questioned us.

Further afield I frequently went to Barley Park, where my Uncle Christopher and my cousins lived. This again was within easy walking distance. I remember once going to ride the pony and, finding there was no saddle, walked back to Witney to get one and

Christopher Bartlett was respected internationally in the beekeeping world.

Everett, the keeper at Barley Park.

Jessie Bartlett and Barry with Beauty, Turk and Sweep in Bartlett's Close.

this we carried back! My mother often walked across the footpaths to Brize Norton to visit her aunt who lived there. At Barley Park we spent a lot of time with the keeper, Everett. With him I was introduced to trapping, shooting and ferreting and, although I did not have a shotgun then, I was occasionally allowed to use his twelve-bore. In trying to reach a moorhen's nest on the pond, I got caught up with my head nearly in the water and was rescued by my father. It was here, also, that my cousin, Denis, shot one of the men in the arm when playing with an air rifle. This was something that was treated very seriously, although I cannot remember what happened to him.

We were brought up with guns and rifles – my grandfather won innumerable prizes at Oxford and Wimbledon. His son, Oswald, won the Queen's Prize at the opening of the range at Witney and another son, Chris, was a sergeant instructor. My Uncle Percy, often known in the family as PB, was the best shot I have ever seen with a shot-gun. We all had air guns and rifles from a very early age but safety was always drilled into us from the start; to point

a gun or use it dangerously was a very serious crime and we were very conscious of this. I kept rabbits (Belgian Hares) and tried to get some pigeons from the pigeon loft at Minster Lovell but I was unable to catch them. There were always dogs, cats and cage birds about; this close contact with animals made me very conscious of their suffering. I do not think many people were intentionally cruel but my expeditions with the keeper brought this home to me.

At Wimbledon, we had a dog, an Aberdeen terrier, which accompanied us when we went to Witney where there were two other dogs, Beauty, a greyhound, owned by my grandfather and Sweep, a black retriever, which belonged to Uncle Joe. Sweep was my special friend, he was always looked on as my dog and went nearly everywhere with me. He lived in a large kennel in the yard but was never tied up. I could not have been very old when I crawled into the kennel when a fight was in progress, to the alarm of my parents.

We had many amusements, sliding on ponds and skating on frozen flood water. Even the Town itself was attractive. There was little or no traffic and one played in the roads and on pavements

Percy Bartlett, 1918.

Barry and Sweep. 1911.

without much hindrance. When we had any money, the most attractive shop was King's where ice cream was made on the premises and cost a halfpenny or penny and where many sweets were available at a cost of a penny for 4 oz – sometimes even 6 oz.

The town was usually quiet but was transformed on market day each Thursday with alternating 'small' and 'big' markets. On big market days the town came alive with cattle, sheep and pigs being driven through the streets. Some of these escaped up yards and alleys and had to be driven out; there was always the hope that some might come up the yard! The Square became full of penned sheep. Horses and carts were all around, implements and other wares were laid out on the bank and there was great activity buying and selling (some of which took place in the pubs). There were people of all ages, farmers and their families, various dealers, corn merchants and the odd cheap jack.

In the Corn Exchange, seed merchants and others had little box desks on legs, with their names painted on them, from which they did their business. It was a day out for a lot of people from the surrounding countryside; they came on foot, on cycles, in floats or traps and by railway. Blacksmiths and shopkeepers did a roaring trade as nearly everyone from the country took the opportunity to have the horse shod or do their shopping but there was still plenty of room to move about the roads and pavements, even in the Market Square. At the railway station to meet most trains was the local bus run by Payne's; this was a box-like four-wheeler entered from the rear and drawn by one horse. It deposited or picked up passengers more or less where they requested in the town. There was always straw on the floor.

When my father was home, which was generally at weekends, he took me with him to golf and on other expeditions. The first golf course I can remember started at Cogges where clubs were kept at the school, and the course played over the main Oxford Road towards Northfield Farm. Later the course was moved to Northfield Farm and an old railway coach was propped up and used as a club house. In this club house bottled lemonade was kept which was always a great attraction to me. The bottles were sealed by a marble or were stoneware with screw tops and cost about a penny each. I looked forward eagerly to these weekends spent with my father and was always hopeful that there would be snow or frost so that we could go skating or tobogganing.

Apart from measles, whooping cough, colds and minor ailments, I can remember no illness and I had no contact with any doctor or dentist in those days. We were singularly free from accidents. I remember only two that made any impression on me. On one occasion my father was thrown from his horse, which had put a foot in a gulley in the Woodstock Road; fortunately my father was not badly hurt. Another accident occurred when tobogganing at Crawley when one of my father's friends damaged his leg against a stone wall.

I remember visiting the cobblers who sat on low stools at the rear of Eaton's and, together with the boys who were with me, put fireworks under the stool of one who was very deaf. A visit to the barbers was a great treat. Two of the local establishments had belt-driven brushes which needed a boy to turn them. We looked forward to having a brush applied to our hair after cutting. It was also an opportunity to look at the comic papers at Whitcher's. The other barber, Burton's, also housed the local telephone exchange which necessitated the barber leaving his shaving or hair cutting to connect a subscriber who wanted to make a call. A hair cut cost twopence.

Although I had learned to ride on my mother's bicycle at Wimbledon, it was some time before I had one of my own and

Sheep pens on 'big' Market Day.

In Bartlett's Close on April 23rd 1912, Barry's birthday, the children from Barley Park and Moorside: Denis, Dorothy (Dorrie), and Bernard tugging against Jessie, Richard Knill (Dick) Bartlett, Phyllis and Barry.

when one was purchased for me at Long's, on the bridge at Witney, I was delighted. My father paid a pound for it and it looked like new with red lining on the frame and plated handle bars. It had only one brake and had possibly started as a fixed wheel. I took it back to Wimbledon where it served me well for some years and where I accompanied my father on journeys into the surrounding countryside as far afield as Epsom, Weybridge, Ewell and Kingston without incident. I was disappointed however that it had no lamp (rear lamps were not thought of) so I saved up some money and bought one for 1/3d. Both my parents strongly disapproved and I was not allowed to use it at night. The end of this lamp came quite soon; I was thrown off when a stick caught in my front wheel and the only thing damaged was the lamp, which seemed to please my father. Roads were almost empty of traffic but the surfaces were generally of grit which caused rapid wear of tyres. There were frequent punctures and potholes and other obstacles abounded.

The garden at Moorside (79 High Street) where my Uncle Percy came to live, was a favoured playground for me and my cousins who lived there and I always entered by climbing over the wall from the yard rather than by the normal entrance. This entry included walking over the roof of the adjoining summerhouse owned by Miss Smith. Although she expressed her resentment, she did not stop me.

I remember: long walks with my mother when I recovered from a bout of measles …. the death of Aunt Nancy, Uncle Joe's wife in 1908….the death of my grandfather in 1910….the journeys in the car with my Uncle Joe who was always very kind and patient with me. The car then was an Adler two-cylinder which had little power but in which we travelled to Aston over the hills; the dusty roads made the hedges white and on them were clouds of goldfinches. At Aston a large stone building was under construction. Other journeys, I can remember, were to a sawmill at Appleton, the Vicarage at South Leigh and, much later on, to Stoke Lyne near Ardley.

Some years later Dick Bartlett in Bartlett's Yard.

My bedroom at Witney was at the back of 71 High Street and looked over the garden; this room had no electric light so when I went to bed I was provided with a candle. I was lulled to sleep by the beat of the single-cylinder gas engine in the generating station at the end of the yard, the sound of which died away when the lights of the town were switched off leaving what load was left to be taken over by the batteries. Then there was complete darkness and silence and the last sounds I heard came from the hooting of the owls in the old yew tree in the garden.

Until the spring of 1913, when I was twelve, Witney was a very important part of my life, I was accepted as part of the local community but I have only patchy general memories of these latter years before being swept into the pattern of public school life. All this is now of course a long, long time ago but when I started my new life at King's College School, it seemed to me that I had left another world behind at Witney.

The Adler two-cylinder (c. 1907/8) with three speed quadrant gear. This was used by Joseph Francis and possibly by his father. It was the car in which Joseph had his serious accident.

The end of an era

For some reason my parents did not return to Wimbledon for some time after I started at King's and in these early days I stayed with the Wards, who lived next door to Elmside. Here I had a large room that combined the functions of bedroom and study but, although I was given every encouragement, I neglected my studies and was rebuked by Mr Ward for reading fiction when I was supposed to be studying. Although I am not sure how long I stayed with the Wards, I have very clear memories of the Ward household. They had a grey parrot which I disliked because it bit me and a ginger cat to which I was indifferent but I was interested in their guns and rifles, they owned an 8-bore duck gun which I was told they used in Ireland. There was a workshop, a darkroom and other activities that interested me but most clearly I remember having to eat macaroni cheese which I disliked.

By contrast, my memories of early days at school are very dim, probably because I was not interested. I can only assume that I was taught something, but much time and effort was devoted to preparation for gymnastic displays and training for Sports Day held at the end of term. This was a great occasion, a social function for parents and friends, which included a military band playing in the open. All this involved much rehearsal with suitable equipment. We were drilled and taught Physical Training (PT) and boxing by an army sergeant who enforced his authority with a short leather

'tawse' which did us no harm. In fact I liked him and remember his name – Sgt. Maj. Bull, of Aldershot Command.

The other important function was Speech Day held in the Great Hall, this also included a gymnastic display. The headmaster (1910-1934) was Herbert Lionel Rogers. Many boys must have benefited from his firm, kindly influence. He was a most efficient organiser and the school ran smoothly during the difficult war years from 1914 to 1918.

In the pre-war days the school was a pleasant place, the sun always seemed to shine and we played much cricket, we also played rugby in the winter but my memories of this are blurred. The summer of 1914 was fine and warm during which we spent many long hot days in the garden at Elmside where the hammock, slung between two trees, provided a place for cool relaxation. One of the faults in the layout of the house was that it had a south-facing larder, as a result my mother was concerned about keeping food fresh in the hot weather. There were no refrigerators and the blocks of ice obtained from the fishmonger had a short life – so, for a short time, we had a meat safe hanging in the north veranda.

During the holidays much time was spent swimming at the local baths and there were other diversions most of them close to home. One journey further afield was a trip to Brighton to visit the Morleys who were staying at the Palace Hotel. This was the occasion when my father persuaded me to dive from the pier into the sea and I can recall the slippery, weed-encrusted supports as I climbed out. When war was declared, during this summer holiday, I had been at King's a little over a year (four terms). Few people then realised that it was the end of an era. I certainly did not appreciate how fortunate I had been to have experienced the pattern of life in those pre-war days and to have been able to take part in such a well ordered school life.

The school buildings, which overlooked the Common, were dominated by the Great Hall and underneath this was the main entrance hall with some eight classrooms flanked on one side by the porter's lodge and ancillary buildings. Beyond this was the gymnasium and a block of temporary classrooms. On the other side of the main building were additional classrooms, the locker room in the adjoining house and with the Head's house at the rear. Beyond this, to the east, was the junior (preparatory) school. This was entirely separate from the main school. The boys did not mix, they wore red caps with a white badge whilst ours were blue with a rampant lion in red. At the rear of the Head's house were tennis courts (cut by a mower pulled by a pony wearing protective boots) and extending as far as the Ridgeway, was a large area of playing fields. Running between the Ridgeway and the Common was a narrow lane which divided the playing fields from an additional area, probably about an acre, used mainly for cricket, in the corner of this was the small-bore rifle range. Bridging the lane and serving both fields was a two-storey pavilion where teas were served on the upper floor. Nearer the school were the fives courts and a newly built science block with changing rooms underneath. The fees for day boys were, I believe, about £100 a year which were, I think, about the same as St. Paul's School where my cousin Jack went. Although both schools produced a very high standard of education I always thought that the general amenities and situation of King's were much better; later on St. Paul's moved into a new school built for them on the other side of the river, at Hammersmith.

At King's the day started with the assembly of the whole school in the Great Hall. There was a roll call of each form, conducted by the prefects during which the masters and Head assembled on the platform. Promptly, at 9 o'clock, the porter in his uniform with shining buttons, closed the doors and stood inside. Prayers were read and announcements made after which everyone went to their classrooms. Of some fifteen masters who taught us, there are very few that I can remember with any clarity but I am grateful to them all, particularly to those of them who gave so much of themselves in their efforts to teach a small boy who made little effort to learn. There was Felton, my form master, both he and Pullein Thompson were officers in the school Officer's Training Corps (OTC), the latter, a Captain; they were the first to go to war after August 1914. I remember also: 'Freddie' Carrodus, a most popular master who always got the best out of any boy …. Price who always smelt strongly of old pipe tobacco but who made Shakespeare's plays interesting …. Duval, a Frenchman …. Walker, who seemed to take a particular interest in me because he knew the Ashby-Joneses who were friends of my parents …. Latham, whom I liked least of all …. one whose name I have forgotten who wore a clerical collar and walked about like a monk and Oglethorpe who took over the command of the OTC after Pullein Thompson left.

All these impressions are somewhat faint but one that is still quite clear is the scramble at the tuck shop which opened for the morning break. Some boys seemed to have plenty of money but for most of us the expenditure of a penny or twopence had to suffice and some boys just stood outside. My particular friend, Edgington, was always prepared to lend me a penny which I duly returned the next day; we got on very well together and as he lived near to us, we came and went together each day. I envied the apparent ease with which he did homework, he learned far more easily than I did and became a prefect before I left.

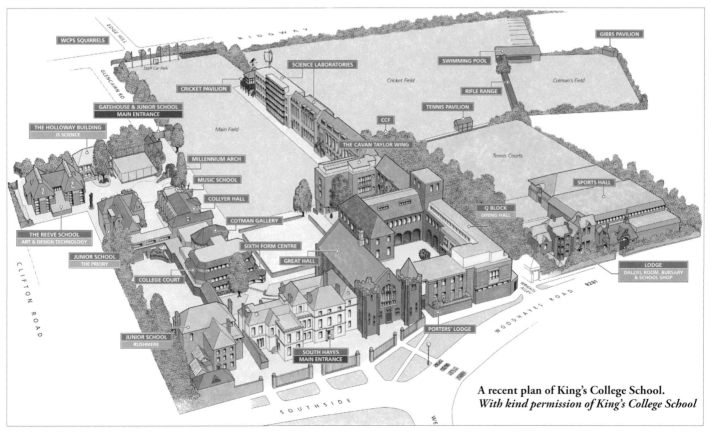

A recent plan of King's College School.
With kind permission of King's College School

On the left, Ernest and Carrie Taylor and towards the right, Jack, Maud, Oswald and Molly Bartlett at Elmside, May 1916.

We watched the burning Zeppelin

My early memories tend to become mixed with later ones that are dominated by the war which broke out just after the commencement of the summer holidays. When I travelled to Witney by train I was unaccompanied, probably for the first time, and I was impressed by the sight of soldiers with fixed bayonets guarding each bridge we passed. All thoughts of war were soon forgotten at Witney but on my return to school there were gaps in the ranks with new faces amongst the masters. The general pattern of life at school continued very much as before during the first months of the war but, as time went on, the grimness of the situation became more and more apparent.

There were alarms and concern about air raids and at one time Uncle Oswald and his family, who lived in London, came over each night to Wimbledon to sleep. From the top floor window at Elmside, we watched the burning Zeppelin which was brought down at Cuffley and after raids I collected shrapnel which was not difficult to find. We suffered no damage at Elmside other than a few tiles broken by shrapnel and Wimbledon had no bomb damage but I cycled over to Streatham to see a large area of houses flattened by bombs. Just north of Elmside, at Coombe Hill, there was a searchlight and an anti-aircraft gun. I used to watch this at practice and no one seemed to take much notice of me when I propped my cycle against the hedge and went inside the enclosure.

There were captive observation balloons at Roehampton and Barnes. Such balloons were a common sight as were cars with a gas bag on top when petrol became short – I even saw a motorcycle with a gas bag on a trailer. In later raids, a warning was given by exploding a maroon and 'all clear' by bugles, a very welcome sound at night.

Food became difficult. In the early years, although it was not rationed, I still remember being hungry. We had a regular box, known as the 'egg box', sent by rail from Witney. Here things seemed much easier and life was still very pleasant with little apparent shortage.

Everyone at school joined the OTC and this training became very serious, in fact it seemed to me to take precedence over everything else. There were frequent parades and we were issued with standard khaki uniform which included puttees; I soon found that what were known as 'Fox's puttees' were much easier to wear and these could be bought. Generally the uniform was, to me, a most uncomfortable and restricting form of dress and I never got used to it.

In the early days, training consisted mainly of parades, drilling and instruction. We had Mauser rifles, some of which were tubed, but very soon the standard .303 Lee Enfield, with bolt action and bayonet was available. By 1915 training had become much more intensive – there were frequent 'field ops', route marches (15–20 miles) and firing practice, some of which was on the range at Wraysbury with .303. On field training we were issued with .303 blanks which were a source of cordite for my own use. Camp was 14 days of concentrated training including night ops and sleeping rough; the Common and Richmond Park were ideal training grounds in all weathers at all times. We certainly had to work. Of course the school OTCs were a fruitful source of almost ready-made soldiers; those boys leaving school who were nearing 'call-up' age very soon found themselves in France. In particular I remember our platoon sergeant, Wilson, whose parents lived in a large house almost opposite the school. He left, I believe, in the summer of 1916 and was killed before Christmas.

I disliked this training intensely. I have pictures in my mind of lying in snow and ice in Richmond Park …. route marches in

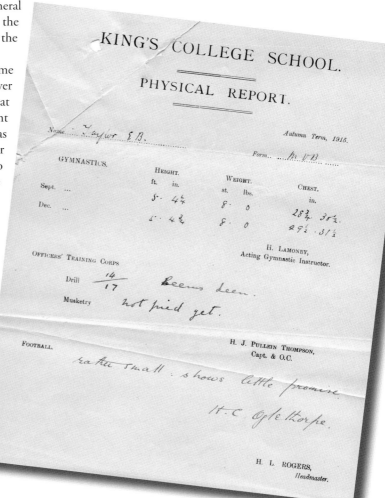

King's College School physical report for Autumn Term 1915.

Boys from King's College School engaged in farm activities at Nutfield Farm near Redhill c. 1915.

blazing sun, falling out and watching Andrews, a drummer in the band, taking off his tiger skin .... guard duty with fixed bayonet for what seemed interminable periods .... trying to find a comfortable spot in gorse while waiting for dawn to break, but nothing that I can recall with any enjoyment or nostalgia. I never achieved any rank in the OTC and my only 'decorations' were an efficiency badge and a marksman's badge but this training has stayed in my mind far more vividly than other activities at school. No doubt there were games and other relaxation but I cannot recall much detail and even the pattern of general school work seems dominated by the OTC. I doubt very much if it was nearly as bad as it seemed.

I am not sure when, but at some period during school holidays, I went to Nutfield (near Redhill) with a party of about twenty boys. We stayed in a large house and helped with various activities on a farm such as haymaking, hoeing and digging. I am not sure what it was all about but doubt if we did much good. I mainly remember the train journey.

As time went on there was a campaign to encourage people to 'dig for victory' and everyone was asked to grow vegetables on whatever ground was available. Trees made the garden at Elmside quite unsuitable so my father dug an area of ground west of the houses in Cottenham Park Road adjoining the old lane. This ground was sour heavy clay, the labour of preparation was Herculean and following the dry hot summer, the product was almost nil. I think that the heartbreaking efforts which he put into this may well have aggravated and hastened the illness that led to his death in 1917.

Barry's final school report 1917.

31

Ernest and Kitty Bartlett in their Wolseley registration 0-162; this was possibly two-cylinder and chain driven. Ernest owned this car when he was at New Brighton where he was the electrical engineer for the tower.

Looking back on the time between 1914 and 1917, a period of only about three years, I tend to see it as a long time during which a great many things happened. No doubt the impressions left in my mind are naturally vivid in parts but I have become a little confused over the timing of some of the happenings. I looked forward avidly to the holiday period. Some of these were spent at Witney which became, in my mind, a sort of paradise of happiness. Certainly the contrast was likely to create this impression because I was transposed from the dull and somewhat spartan conditions of wartime school to a house that seemed full of friendly people, where there was unlimited food and everything that I enjoyed.

The surroundings of the house at 71 High Street have never lost their attraction to me: the peaceful garden with its smells and fruit in the sunshine, the renewal of acquaintance with Forester and Busby, the various animals, visits to 75 and 79 High Street to see my uncles, aunts and cousins, all are still vivid and nostalgic to me and at Christmas the house seemed full of people. There was always a large home-cured ham, to the delight of my father and Uncle Ern, and a lavish display of all kinds of food which must have needed much preparation. Looking back, one wonders how so many people got into a relatively small house, who did all the catering and all the other work that made everything run so smoothly.

The tower at New Brighton – but that is another story!

The train fare from Paddington to Witney was about six shillings. In order to avoid this it was decided that, I believe at Easter in 1916, that Uncle Oswald, my cousin Jack and I should cycle to Witney. We set off from Brook Green early on Good Friday. I think at that time I was using my father's Raleigh, a heavy, three-speed machine with a chain case. There was a strong south-west wind blowing in our faces. Uncle Oswald decided to take a train before we got to Beaconsfield, Jack gave up and got a train at High Wycombe but I continued, probably because I had no money. I arrived tired but triumphant in the evening. This was the forerunner of many journeys to Witney by cycle. On some I was accompanied by Jack and we had many adventures; his cycle frequently broke down and once I towed him from Wheatley to Oxford attached by string. There were many punctures and once I narrowly escaped being run down by a car on the old Dashwood Hill.

The main road to London from Oxford at Dashwood Hill c. 1916.

The road west of Uxbridge was so bad that it was almost impossible to cycle over it but in spite of this I recall being warned by the police that we must not ride on the footpath! The roads generally were narrow and some of the surfaces were very poor. The term 'good' or 'bad' roads is a matter of comparison – most roads were passable but the lack of repair during the war was beginning to show. On many the surface had gone and there were potholes, some of them quite deep; it was necessary for a cyclist to pick a way through them. Some of the surfaces were also very loose in dry weather and the flint or gravel was hard on tyres.

In and around London most of the main roads were surfaced with wood blocks or granite setts and these, with the many tram lines, produced a surface that could be very dangerous as soon as it became wet. All the buses had solid tyres and were difficult to control on this surface. The drivers became expert in correcting skids and I think I owe my life to one in the Fulham Road where,

after I had fallen off my cycle between the tram lines, a bus managed to avoid me and the cycle, by correcting a broadside skid and passing on the pavement. As the result of another skid in the widest part of Kensington High Street I travelled so far on my seat that I lost a large area of my trousers and skin!

These surface conditions were accepted as normal. I well remember the original Auto Carriers (ACs) being almost uncontrollable on wet surfaces; they were famous for their propensity to skid. Many of these were to be seen in the vicinity of Kensington and were used extensively for light delivery by Barkers and Derry & Toms. They consisted of a large box container mounted on a chassis with three wheels, the back one driven through a gearbox by a single-cylinder motorcycle over which the driver sat; he steered the two front wheels with a tiller.

I have retained other memories of this period such as Waterloo Station with troop trains leaving …. helping to make aids for the wounded by shaping wooden handles for walking sticks and crutches …. amateur theatricals in a hut in Durham Road …. hearing the son of Charles Dickens read extracts from his father's books …. trying to thaw frozen pipes with hot water …. skating for what seemed many weeks on the lakes on the Common and on the Serpentine …. people on leave staying at Elmside, in particular my cousins Bren Madeley, in his naval uniform, and Aubrey, with crutches and a wounded foot …. hearing an account of Herbert Ward's adventures with the Naval Reserve before he was interned in Holland. All this was part of life during these early war years.

Bren Madeley.

I had other interests too. I have already alluded to my interest in firearms and explosives and to the construction of boats, aircraft and other models (mostly crudely built). For some time I had an ambition to acquire a pedal-driven car in which I thought I could install an engine but this never materialised. I was fascinated by electricity and spent much time at a shop in Kingston called the Economic Electric Company (EEC) where I gained some knowledge but spent little money. I acquired or made many models and, with some danger, played about with mains wiring in the house; one source of supply was to stick pins through the insulation to make contact with the wire.

At an early age I was given a box camera and for some years I used this, developing the films under the stairs by the light of a red oil lamp and making prints by daylight, glazed on a sheet of glass. Later I acquired other cameras and apparatus. Several were plate cameras and one, a gift from my Uncle Percy, was a very good quarter-plate folding camera with an excellent lens with which I did a lot of work. One other that I remember was an Ensignette, a small folding film camera which cost about a pound. To get this sum of money was not easy, but eventually my grandmother said that she would provide it if I learned by heart some long passages from hymns that she thought I should know. I had to work hard to get them word perfect but having succeeded, I immediately cycled to Oxford and bought the camera – which was never much use.

Equipment was not easy to get and much of it was home made. My dark room was in the tank room under the roof at Elmside. There was no sink but I made a bench and got rid of waste liquid into a large funnel attached to a hose that discharged under the eaves (to the danger of anyone below). After much experimenting, I succeeded in making an enlarger which produced some very good results. This consisted of the plate camera attached to the front of a box which was constructed to enclose a condenser and an electric light bulb. The acquisition of the condenser was difficult but eventually I found a poor quality lens of sufficient size and the right focal length which I purchased for 1/- in Holborn. This worked quite well but all the equipment was very crude and even the 'ground glass' was made by etching with suitable acid over a lead tray. However, I got a lot of experience and enjoyment and, considering the equipment, I think I produced some quite good results.

As the war progressed the increasing shortage of manpower on farms became more obvious and it was suggested that I might drive a tractor during the holidays. Although I greeted the idea with enthusiasm, it never came to be and I doubt very much if my inexperienced efforts would have been much help with the crude machines that then existed.

My father had a Wall Auto-Wheel fitted to a cycle that he used. This consisted of a small pneumatic-tyred wheel in a frame that carried a small four-stroke petrol engine in a unit, complete with petrol tank and driving the wheel by a chain. The whole was attached to the offside rear of the cycle by a spindle forming the fulcrum on which the unit was free to move up or down and traction was provided by its own weight. It was an effective motive power to a cycle but it was rather hard on the cycle and needed better brakes than those provided. Speeds of over 20 mph could be obtained. On occasions in the evenings, I was allowed to use it and on this contraption I tore around the local roads keeping my eyes open for any sign of a policeman, because I had no licence to drive it!

The Wall Auto-Wheel at Wimbledon 1917.

Although the period prior to the war was in complete contrast to that after August 1914, the first years were not nearly so spartan as those after 1916. To a great extent life went on in the general pattern of the pre-war era; my father still obtained his hand-made 'Memphis' cigarettes and his selection of special cigars and apart from air raid scares, shortage of some foodstuffs and some restrictions, it did not seem to me that we lacked very much.

After about 1916, however, most people realised how serious the position had become. This was brought home in many ways. My mother did not have any help in the house, many luxuries disappeared and there was a constant reminder of the increasing shortage of manpower.

At the end of 1916, I went to Witney with my parents and we enjoyed the usual Christmas festivities which seemed little affected by the war. As usual we stayed with my grandmother at 71 High Street where there was the same family gathering of my uncles, aunts and cousins. In January, my father took me to an amateur pantomime which was held in the Corn Exchange and I was greatly attracted by the leading lady. I think this terminated the holiday and I remember being reluctant to return to Wimbledon and to start the new term at school. However, I went back with my father. For some reason my mother did not return with us and we spent a few days looking after ourselves, as there was no maid. Nearly all middle class households had some domestic help in those days and I have a shadowy memory of a series of maids and helps back to the days at Thames Ditton. Generally they left little impression on me although I think the last one was Sophie who came from an orphanage.

There followed a period of very cold weather and the frost lasted several weeks. It was a trying winter. The only means of heating was the range in the kitchen and the open fires. As a result the pipes in the roof and the tanks froze. There was a long period of skating on the lakes and ponds on the Common and we walked long distances.

For the first time in my life I remember feeling ravenously hungry – the shortage of food was beginning to be felt – all sorts of substitutes were produced, even for bread. I can still taste strawberry jam made without sugar and with salt added to keep it.

It was a long dreary winter and the OTC training was most distasteful to me with field ops in Richmond Park and on the Common. In the spring my father worked hard on the vegetable patch. In May he showed the first signs of the illness which culminated in his death and he became rapidly worse with what was diagnosed as a gastric ulcer. There is little doubt that if present-day medical knowledge had then been available, his life could have been saved or at least prolonged but no remedy or hospital treatment was even suggested and he died quite peacefully on June 11th at the age of fifty. A few hours before he died he talked to me quite calmly, gave me advice and said "Look after your mother my boy". The quotation chosen by my mother and inscribed over his grave is a very fitting tribute to him; this was – "E'en as he strode that day to God so walked he from his birth in simpleness and gentleness and honour and clean mirth."

The day of the funeral was very hot. I have in my mind a picture of what was, I suppose, a typical funeral of that period. The hearse with horses draped and with black plumes that nodded when they moved and horse-drawn carriages all moving slowly along the road to Morden. Through the window, I could see passers-by removing their hats and everyone dressed in deep black mourning but I have no memory whatever of the service at the cemetery.

So ended the first chapter of my life – a period of security and contentment – a period during which I did not appreciate how fortunate I was or realise until later how well I was cared for by my parents.

Ernest Taylor.

Caroline Taylor.

Chelsea supply station, Alpha Place c.1900.

Part Two
FINDING MY WAY

My rides seem to have been of an exploratory nature

Although I was aware of the great loss we had suffered by my father's death, this did not affect my immediate outlook to any very great extent, as with the resilience of youth I looked forward with enthusiasm to the immediate future. My father had expressed a wish that I should have the Auto-Wheel that he used and I was excited at the prospect of being allowed to use it. I was in fact encouraged to do so; it did not require any tax and my Uncle Percy provided me with the money to obtain a driving licence. Petrol was difficult to get but I found that after warming up and the use of extra air, it would run on paraffin. Although I never ventured far afield, I had much enjoyment on it around Wimbledon and Kensington – and several nasty spills on greasy roads. Eventually I sold it for, I think, about £10 to Myson (a friend of Uncle Oswald) in Cromwell Road.

After my father's death my mother faced many problems, not the least of which was that of finance. My father had never accumulated much money, his shares in Alfred Chapman had depreciated considerably owing to the war and in any case they were, like all private company shares, almost unsaleable. The Company continued to pay his director's salary for a while but the only real asset we had was the house, Elmside at Wimbledon, and my schooling was costly. Obviously, we must sell or let the house and I must try to earn a living. Here my mother made a very wise decision in deciding to go away, to think things over and talk with her relatives. The house would produce an income if it was let furnished, we could live somewhere else and I thought I should be able to earn a wage although I had no clear ideas of what I wanted to do. Anyway, she decided to go and stay at Wigston and at the end of the summer term she went by train whilst I cycled.

I remember this ride in some detail. It was the longest I had embarked on in one day and because I lost my way, the distance shown on my cyclometer was over 120 miles by the time I reached Wigston. I started before five in the morning and rode across the Common to Barnes, over Hammersmith Bridge via Kensington to Edgeware Road and on to Cricklewood which was little more than a village. Here I watched Handley-Page aircraft from the side of the road near a small group of shops facing the aerodrome and everything seemed quite rural. There was little traffic – a few horses and carts and a very occasional motor lorry – these were quite slow and it was possible to hold on to the side and get a tow which I often did.

On through St. Albans and Dunstable, beyond which I decided to add a little air to my tyres, really for no reason at all because everything was going well. It proved a great mistake because the day was becoming warm and towards Fenny Stratford my back tyre exploded with a loud report. This was a disaster; I had to walk back several miles. Fortunately I had enough money to buy another tyre and afterwards I made good progress towards Daventry during the

St. Wolstans, Wigston Magna, Leicestershire.

William and Allie Morley (née Knock).

afternoon. Here I made another mistake and took the wrong road travelling some extra miles before reaching Blaby, where I still had difficulty in finding the way to Wigston. I eventually arrived tired and triumphant about eight in the evening.

I soon forgot my troubles. The house at Wigston always seemed full of friendly people who were staying or visiting. Aunt Allie welcomed everyone and was full of fun in spite of Uncle Will's disabilities; he was a relation on my father's side. Although he had a rather forbidding presence, he was always very kind to me and I liked him. His wife, Aunt Allie, was my grandmother Bartlett's sister and we were therefore doubly related.

Their house, St. Wolstans, was large with an imposing, though seldom used, entrance from the road. At the rear were farm buildings and the farm, which was let. The normal approach to the house was through the farm entrance at the side and thence to the back door. There was a large kitchen garden away from the house beyond the farm buildings and this suffered much damage from rabbits. After some hesitation my uncle let me use his shotgun and when I promptly returned with a rabbit, I was allowed to have the gun at any time and spent many happy hours walking the fields with Tom Lomas. Previously, on another visit, my uncle had trusted me with his air pistol which I had jammed and Aunt Allie had taken it to Leicester to get it cleared – to my great relief.

After a short stay at Wigston we decided to go on to Canley where the Madeleys had a small farm. This lay about a mile and a half from Coventry just off the Kenilworth Road in completely rural surroundings and was approached from the main road through a water splash. The whole area of the farm with the house, buildings and surroundings is now (at the time of writing) covered by the factory which was built by the Standard Motor Company, later

A family gathering at Wigston: Standing, Will Morley and Roy Madeley. Middle row, Thomas Lomas, Myfanwy Hughes, Allie Morley and Amy Madeley. On the ground, Percy Bartlett, Fred Knock and Ernest Bartlett.

known as Canley Works. I cycled from Wigston to a railway station at Coventry where I had arranged to meet my mother from her train and, carrying our luggage, we walked to the farm at Canley.

Here there was unlimited cream from the milk left to set in pancheons in the dairy and this we enjoyed together with unlimited fruit from the garden. I rode on one of the horses using the grass verges of the main Kenilworth Road for gallops and for the first (and only) time I rode on a side-saddle. Bren Madeley was on leave from the Navy and I remember an occasion when he took me with him to Coventry where we visited a pub. This was my first introduction to the inside of one, and I can't remember if I drank anything but I soon tired of being there and got bored with the company. I decided to walk home without him. I lost my way in the dark and I arrived at Canley very late in the evening but even so, I was asleep when Bren arrived back.

While we were staying at Canley I went with my mother to Coventry where we met someone who was, I believe, an assistant manager of the Daimler car factory. At this time Coventry was the centre of the motor car manufacturing industry; Daimler, Wolseley and Humber were some of the larger concerns whilst William Morris was almost unknown. I believe it was through my uncle at Wigston that we got the appointment and I remember the interview only vaguely. I had little or no idea of what I wanted to do or what type of work I might be involved in, but I explored various other possibilities of employment including driving agricultural tractors and wireless telegraphy.

As far as I can remember, there was never any suggestion that I should have anything to do with the building industry and it never occurred to me that there might be any opening in this for me. I did not treat any of this quest for work very seriously – I was still a schoolboy and both work and the future seemed very remote – I was more concerned with the prospect of holidays at Witney and after a short stay at Canley we made our way there.

The cycle ride through Kenilworth and Warwick was pleasant and easy and the day was fine but again I lost my way. I remember going through Chipping Norton and enquiring how to get to Witney. My map reading must have been very poor and probably consisted of picking out the main towns on the route and my rides seem to have been of an exploratory nature with enquiries from place to place as I went along. In spite of all the delays my average speed was probably around ten miles per hour. I seemed to be able to get to my destination in about the time anticipated with the journey from Canley to Witney taking about six hours. The roads were bad with poor surfaces and the cycle I used had belonged to my father, it was the heavy Raleigh with a three-speed hub and chain case and was probably loaded with luggage so that average speed I achieved was quite passable. I have very clear memories of my arrival at Witney about teatime on a fine sunny day where I was welcomed by my grandmother and refreshed with boiled eggs and bread and butter.

Thoughts of getting a job and earning a living faded away and I was content to enjoy the atmosphere of the house and the people surrounding me, all of which had become so much a part of holidays at Witney. It was not of course the place but the associations that attracted me: the friendly atmosphere at the house where my grandmother lived …. the maid who attended to my wants …. the other houses I visited and looked on as homes …. Aunt Nan at 75 and Auntie Blanche at 79 …. Forester in the garden …. Busby in the yard …. the horses and my dog Sweep who was always there to welcome me. All these held a very high place in my affections.

Percy and Blanche Bartlett at Moorside, 79 High Street.

Forester in the garden.

My dog Sweep – 'always there to welcome me'.

During this stay at Witney I was given the task of making a large pair of doors to replace those, that had become rotten, at the entrance from the road at the lower end of the garden at Elmside. This was quite an undertaking for me on my own but it was good experience. Eventually I got them finished and primed and they were sent by rail and carrier to Wimbledon. When we returned I hung them, again as far as I can remember, entirely alone. I am now surprised that I ever succeeded in doing this. This entrance was also used by a neighbour who possessed a Wolseley Stellite car of about 1912 or 13 vintage. I took a great interest in this and believe he acquired it about the same time that Morris first marketed his car with a White & Poppe engine. After hanging the doors, I also painted the roof and other woodwork of the conservatory with white lead; this may have planted the seeds of my dislike for any form of painting!

It had been decided that I should complete the next term at school and leave at Christmas and my mother had taken steps to let the house furnished, from some time in October. When we vacated the house we went to live in some rooms in Cambridge Road in a house at the far end, near the junction with Coombe Lane. I have only a dim memory of the rooms in Cambridge Road but it was here that I read in the papers that tanks had been used at Cambray, on the Somme, for the first time. There was a general atmosphere of depression, we were in the fourth year of the war, my father had died and we had moved into strange surroundings. The outlook seemed bleak.

When I left school at the end of the term in December, my education was far from complete and I was without any real idea of what I wanted to do. The Head, Lionel Rogers, took the trouble to talk to me and give me advice that was sound but which, at the time, made little impression. When I left I severed all my connections and associations with Wimbledon; I was only too glad to escape from the controls of school life and the intensive OTC training which I disliked so much. I had no real regrets at the time but I have since often regretted that I did not keep in touch with some of the friends I knew there. However, I had to get a job of some sort and I gave no more thought to past associations. It was many years before I took any interest as an 'old boy' in the activities of King's College School. I did not even maintain any connection with my great friend Edgington.

A career in electrical engineering seemed attractive

I did not realise, at the time, how much help and advice I received from my Uncle Oswald who was also my Godfather; it was he who suggested that a career in electrical engineering might be suitable and it was agreed that I should start work at Kensington in January 1918. He held a position of some importance with the Kensington & Knightsbridge Electricity Supply Company as Resident Engineer and the area under his control was quite extensive.

The main generating station was situated at Wood Lane, Shepherds Bush, and from here current was fed at 5,000 volts to rotary converters at Kensington Court, Albert Vaults and Cheval Place which covered the whole of the Kensington, Knightsbridge, Notting Hill and Brompton areas. The entrance to Kensington Court was over a weighbridge that had been in use when coal was delivered to the steam generators which had originally provided the supply of electricity. Later the supply was provided by motor generators or rotary converters which then consisted of four 180 kW Orkelons and two 300 kW sets later increased by two 500 kW Bruce Peebles

The battery room, Kensington Court.

Kensington Court generators, 1917.

in the large top room where we were frequently aroused by air-raid warnings, in the form of maroons, and had to make our way down to the cellars under the kitchen, the floor of which had been covered with thick steel plates. Here, together with the maid, Edith Kinchen, and the cat we spent many long hours during the worst raids.

I was given every opportunity to learn by those with whom I associated: some of them I still remember with affection .... Williams, Uncle Oswald's deputy with whom I spent a lot of time and who helped me in every way .... Roberts, an assistant engineer .... Gammage, a foreman .... Fortescue, a fitter .... Walters, a battery attendant .... Chaundler, a clerk .... Ballard, Coppings and Harrison, senior shift engineers at the Court and many others are amongst those that I can still visualise.

I worked in the test room and absorbed knowledge of workshop practice. I visited other stations and worked in the office on logs, records and calculations. I helped the fitters and did a night shift on the generating floor. Not only did this provide me with an insight into all the aspects of the electrical side but at the same time I gained knowledge of other engineering skills. I used my hands and sometimes got really dirty. I remember a visit to Thames Ditton when Mr Hart seemed aghast that I should be working with my hands – but all in all this period of training was invaluable. I am sure that real practical experience and 'know-how' are invaluable possessions for anyone and particularly for those who are likely to assume a position of authority.

The test room, Kensington Court 1917.

converters which distributed at 220 volts with 400 volts between outer cables. The Albert Vaults station housed motor generators of a rather larger total output and a similar battery. Some old steam generators driven by triple expansion Willans engines were still left at Cheval Place but they were disused and I believe this station was closed when Pelham Street was opened and became the Company headquarters. There were batteries at all the stations, I have forgotten the capacity of the cells but they were very large and the total weight of lead must have been terrific. All the generators were at Kensington Court with the distribution department at the Vaults.

The Court offices were on three floors and on the top floor were those of the managing director, Mr Millar, and the Resident Engineer; adjacent to these and opening onto the flat roof over the battery room was the test room. This was really a small well-equipped workshop, which also contained much electrical measuring equipment.

After spending Christmas at Witney, I packed my bags and travelled to London by train to start work at Kensington Court in January 1918 as test room assistant for which I was paid about 3/6 a week. Obviously here I had the opportunity of learning a great deal and the opportunity also of a career in electrical engineering which seemed attractive to me. I have always felt a deep sense of gratitude to my uncle for the trouble he took to look after me and to guide me, so very wisely, in those early days.

At first I lived with him and my aunt, with Jack and Molly, at 40 Aynhoe Road and I was always made to feel that it was my home and that I was part of the family. I am afraid, at the time, I took it all for granted and it never entered my head to express any appreciation for the way I was made welcome in their home. Jack and I had beds

Somewhat reluctantly, I attended evening classes at the Polytechnic at Chelsea where I suppose I learnt some theory. I travelled by bus, getting some food at a coffee stall, to save going home and sheltering in the Underground when there was a raid. Although buses were always available we did not use them when there was time to walk or cycle. There was a good service, buses were cheap and reliable, you could go a long way for a penny and seldom had to wait more than a few minutes for an appropriate bus. I can still remember most of the route numbers; the 49 down Church Street ran to Chelsea and 27, 33 and 9 covered the journey from Hammersmith to Kensington. They seldom stopped running even in raids. After the war some of the buses were replaced by 'lorry buses'; these were army lorries with access via a short ladder let down at the rear. They had bench seats and provided a shattering ride!

I remember the spring of 1918 as a period of distressing news of the war. Everywhere were placards displaying the news of the German offensive and proclaiming further advances towards Paris. There was great anxiety.

The staff of Kensington Court on a 'bean-feast'; centre right Oswald Bartlett with his coat over his shoulder.

In the early summer, my mother came to London and took some rooms in Rowan Road and here we lived until she was able to rent a house, 38 Anyhoe Road, next to Uncle Oswald's house at 40 Aynhoe Road. This house was furnished and provided a home for us until the owner returned after the war ended; we also looked after the cat. The previous house in Rowan Road had been sunny with a small pleasant garden and I remember the scent of flowers through the open window of my bedroom. In contrast, 38 Aynhoe Road seemed cold and depressing but it provided a home conveniently at a very small cost. From the rear windows was the view of a sea of wooden barrels; the area was owned by Lyons, the caterers, and I was told that the barrels contained material for the manufacture of margarine. Food rationing was becoming more stringent but the war news had greatly improved. On one occasion my mother and I were invited to lunch with the Pixleys at Woking. They were bullion brokers in the City and I was duly impressed with their affluent way of life; A cousin, Roy Madeley had recently become engaged to their daughter Violet.

As the date for call-up of my age group drew nearer, I thought I might be able to avoid being drafted into the army by volunteering for some other type of service. I had an intense dislike of any army training because of my experience with the school OTC and I was prepared to try anything else. The Marconi Wireless Telegraph Co. employed sea-going operators whose uniform had a certain amount of glamour that attracted me and I thought my electrical experience would be useful, but my application through normal sources was turned down. I got my Uncle Ern to use some influence with the Houston Shipping Line with which he had connections, and this was successful in getting my application accepted. When it became clear that the war was almost over, I withdrew the application but I felt guilty in doing so because my uncle must have asked favours and pulled strings to get the acceptance.

At this time there was prevalent a particularly virulent type of influenza and many people became very ill without much warning. Many died from it including my Great Uncle Christopher at Witney. I remember feeling very ill when walking from Hammersmith to Brook Green and having difficulty in getting home.

One Saturday, early in November 1918, I walked to Holborn to see the Lord Mayor's Show and had an excellent view from the top of a horse-drawn trolley. There were few people there but they displayed a mood of cheerful optimism that the war was nearly over. On November 11th at 11.00 a.m. the maroons signalled the end of hostilities. The rejoicings of the population of London on this day are well known and I was in the middle of it all. I walked through Kensington and Knightsbridge past the Albert Hall and on to Brompton Road and Piccadilly, up Haymarket and the Mall to Buckingham Palace. This was the London I knew and I took part in the rejoicings everywhere. When I returned late in the evening I had been on my feet all day but felt no sign of tiredness. The memory of that day stays with me.

The following Summer I remember also the Peace celebrations and the firework display in Hyde Park but this is only a dim memory and by this time there was a certain amount of disillusionment after demobilisation and I cannot recall much enthusiasm or rejoicing.

William Christopher Bartlett, who died 12th October 1918.

It seemed like waking from a bad dream

Soon after the armistice, Major Lowe and his family wanted to move back into 38 Aynhoe Road so my mother rented a flat in Rugby Mansions. This was in a block of flats at the rear of the main Hammersmith Road, almost opposite Addison Road Station and Olympia. It was on the ground floor, sparsely furnished and almost sunless; I think the rent was about 30/- a week. Here we spent the rest of the winter and I have memories of depressing surroundings, poor lighting in foggy streets after the blackout and a cold uninviting building. The war was over, Armistice rejoicings had died away; it seemed like waking after a bad dream but no one expected their world to alter immediately and there was no quick return to peacetime conditions.

Those who came back and those who had suffered did not have much to say and those of us not directly involved did not ask many questions. Those who had died were still fresh in our memories. They were of my generation and of my world and we who grow old have the privilege of still remembering. We are the inheritors of the consequences of a war which Paul Johnson in *Offshore Islanders* termed the greatest moral, spiritual and physical catastrophe in the entire history of the English people. Are we to forget the long destruction which claimed the lives of millions?

I was confirmed on December 10th 1918. Before we left Anyhoe Road we spent Christmas at Witney meeting the family. I have a faint memory of sitting down to a loaded table and watching my Uncle Ern carve a ham and expecting him to make some comment about my change of mind about the Marconi Company. However, little was said that I can remember. At this time I was more interested in getting myself another cycle to ride. I still had my father's old Raleigh and I gave much thought to changing this. It was very heavy and the brakes were a frequent trouble. They were operated by cables running inside the handlebars and frame from inverted levers and the bare cables were difficult to keep in place and adjust. After considering several alternatives, I eventually exchanged the Raleigh for another machine of the same make. This was a light roadster with smaller wheels and a single speed and on this I travelled many, many trouble-free miles.

About the same time I bought my first motor cycle for £16. This was a single-cylinder FN (Fabrique Nationale de Herstal) with a shaft drive; I pushed it from York Road, Battersea to Rugby Mansions one evening on a dark and foggy night. It was in poor condition and I had to do a lot of work on the universal joint to the shaft. I had the advantages of the use of the test room workshop and in addition I was able to make use of a building in a mews near Gloucester Place where my uncle and Mr Miller kept their cars. I had a free run of this at any time. On the ground floor was ample room for two or three cars and a bench and tools, but no machinery. It had been used as a feeder station and stores but was no longer needed. It was the usual type of mews building with two floors, double doors for a carriage and a single entrance with a circular staircase inside.

Uncle Oswald's Adler was a two-seater with dickey, dating from about 1912 and the other was an open four-seater, made about the same date, by the White Steam Car Co. This had an orthodox petrol engine and a four speed gearbox with an overdrive to a geared up top. On these two cars I learned a lot and short of starting them up on my own, I was allowed to do what I liked and

Oswald Bartlett's four-cylinder c.1912 Adler which he bought about 1914 and sold in 1919. In this car Barry learned to drive. In the picture, it is parked outside Oswald's house in Aynhoe Road, London with Molly seated inside.

43

I soon familiarised myself with the movements of driving without going onto the road. In fact I have no memory of ever having any driving instruction but one day when my uncle was taken ill at Brook Green, he asked me if I thought I could drive his car back to the garage. Of course I said 'yes' and I drove it through Kensington, down Palace Gate and Gloucester Place and into the mews. It was getting dark and the lights bothered me but my only trouble was getting it into the garage because of the narrow entrance and I touched one hood iron on the door frame, leaving a groove. I never forgot the lesson in turning into a narrow opening. I am still amazed that my uncle should have entrusted me with his car and he must have had surprising confidence in my ability because I cannot remember ever driving the car when he was with me. A little later, at Witney, he asked me to drive the car to Ducklington at night, with only oil lamps, to help someone get to Barley Park and I remember how difficult it was to see where I was going.

I did not keep the FN very long, as all sorts of troubles became apparent and I sold it for £18. By this time I had managed to amass a small amount of capital. I had £15.18.3 in the Savings Bank plus a few pounds in a War Loan and some cash and I soon bought another motor cycle. In this connection I learned not to place any trust in deposits; I agreed to buy a Triumph at Peckham for £14 and left a deposit until I could fetch it, only to find next day when I went, that it had been sold for more money. However, at Kilburn I found a De Dion that was very old (about 1903) but sound, I pushed it home having paid about £6 for it. Originally it had a surface carburettor and this had been replaced by a B & B (Brown and Barlow) but it retained the original coil ignition and ran quite well. I did not keep it long and sold it for £11 to an American. I considered several other motor cycles but for some reason my enthusiasm waned and during the spring and summer of 1919 I did all my travelling on my Raleigh cycle.

In April of this year we left Addison Road and my mother went to Witney. I was installed in rooms at 58 Sterndale Road which was adjacent to Brook Green. Here I had a large room at the top of the house and was looked after by a Mrs Davie for which I paid about 30/- a week with full board. She was a widow with two sons, recently demobilised, and a daughter. They were a hard working Scottish family, all older than I was, and Mrs Davie, with the help of a 'daily', looked after me extremely well. I seldom saw the others or the one other lodger who had a small room on the same floor as mine and most of my meals were brought up to my room which was spacious and faced south. In the winter I sometimes had early breakfast in the ground floor front room which I could use if I wished and it was warmer. On the intermediate floor was the bathroom, made from a large bedroom, and here I kept my cycle, carrying it back up a flight of stairs each time I returned home. I was extremely happy there, Mrs Davie looked after me like a mother, I was fed well and it was clean and I could use the room as I wished. In fact, I did quite a lot of photography by using a developing box and printing by gaslight. The light was a gas bracket fitted with a mantle and I had a good coal fire. In warm summer weather, although there were three large sash windows, the room got very hot at night after almost all day sun.

During the summer of 1919 I did a lot of cycling and made frequent trips to Witney at weekends and any holiday period I could manage. The weekends usually started after Saturday midday and I returned Sunday evening but more than once I rode back early Monday morning starting from Witney at about 2.00 a.m. and getting to work by 9.00 a.m.

Coming back from a weekend at Shoreham, where Uncle Oswald had a holiday bungalow, one Sunday night I fell into an unlit trench across the road at Croydon. This did a little damage to the cycle but I was unhurt. Another accident involved a collision with a delivery van at the rear of Kensington Court. My back wheel was so buckled that it had to be entirely rebuilt, the cost of which was defrayed by Slatter's, the provision merchants.

In May of this summer Uncle Oswald decided to sell his car. Prices had risen to a very high level after the war, an Auto Carrier (AC) open two-seater cost over £500. He sold it to someone who lived in a large

Barry's accommodation at 58 Sterndale Road, London.

Oswald's next Adler car which he later sold to his brother Joseph in about 1921; Barry drove this car for many miles.

house next to Strachan and Brown, the coachbuilders, at the corner of Earls Court Road for £360; he did not buy another for some time although I went with him to look at several. He must have had something to use because he travelled to Shoreham and other places; perhaps he had the use of Mr Miller's 'White'? He bought another Adler, with a wide two- or three-seater but no dickey. In December we did a lot of work on this, I remember fitting new pistons and I turned the rings in the test room lathe.

I enjoyed the summer and, as well as going to Shoreham, I spent Easter, Whitsun and Summer holidays at Witney. For some reason, in September I went to Wigston by train and was caught by the railway strike which took place while I was there. I had some difficulty in getting back but eventually completed the journey packed into a guard's van.

I think it must have been during this visit that I was introduced to a curate who was a friend of the Madeleys. For some reason which I can no longer remember, I agreed to exchange my Raleigh cycle for his Swift. It was a very poor exchange from my point of view. I had not seen the Swift until it arrived by train and I never liked it. I do not remember ever using it for any long-distance rides and I regretted parting from the Raleigh which had served me so well.

My memories of Sterndale Road are in complete contrast to those of Addison Road. The first summer was long and sunny, I went about a lot and my days were always full. On one rare occasion there was a party at Aynhoe Road where I was one of a lot of young people who enjoyed the, then, unusual entertainment of a gramophone. I

sat next to a girl named Mary Study (but she was soon forgotten). I remember being fascinated by the strains of gramophone music coming from near my room in Sterndale Road and, in my young and rose-coloured view, all the world seemed gay, everyone was full of hope for the future and the privations of the war were forgotten. I smoked a pipe, not because I really liked it but because it seemed a manly thing to do. I had started smoking regularly when I was about seventeen but my uncle had convinced me that a pipe was better than cigarettes and I seldom used them. Tobacco cost about tenpence an ounce and, like all youngsters, I tried all kinds. It never entered my head to drink alcohol but I smoked quite a lot and Jack Hughes, who was a great friend of mine, taught me how to fill and light my pipe while riding a motor cycle.

Towards the end of 1919 there was considerable activity at the works in connection with the replacement of generating plant and my uncle made several journeys to Scotland to visit the Bruce Peebles works: I had little to do with this but I was kept busy in the test room on experiments with High Tension (HT) fuses and coil windings, vibration tests and so on. I have no clear picture of any particular happenings in the works at this time although there must have been much activity in replacing some of the cumbersome and outdated generating plant which had seen service for so long before the war.

Preparation for the removal to Pelham Street as well as the reorganisation of mains and feeders all over the area must have been well to the fore but I have retained only the impressions made on me by the happenings in my own little world. Even here, my memory is not always infallible. I can remember no friction in relationship with the workmen and it was a happy community. There was no form of canteen and the most that was provided was a boiling ring and possibly a kettle. Shift workers brought their own food and I have seen kippers being cooked on a shovel in the fire of a small vertical boiler. In the test room we had a kettle and a few odd cups and sometimes, when we could afford it, a tin of sweet condensed milk. Two holes were punched in the top of the tin and blowing down one, produced milk from the other; the tin could be sealed afterwards with wooden plugs placed in the holes. One of the shift hands, Arlott, told me many stories of the time when he was employed as an assistant driver at Cheval Place station. He was paid 37/- a week and said "Believe me, Cheval Place was a very busy place in winter with horse-drawn carts weighing in all day and stokers sweating at the boilers all for about 1500 kW". He had a vast fund of stories such as when Fortescue, the foreman, invited a young labourer with unruly hair, to dip his comb in shellac to 'fix' it – it took half a gallon of methylated spirits to 'unfix' it! On one occasion Roberts offered to top up Mr Bartlett's radiator on his car and fetched a jug of 'distilled water' from the battery room. When the jug was returned someone told him it had contained sulphuric acid – panic stations ensued and a wash out with soda water. No one said anything about it! Everywhere was warm in winter because there was an efficient system of steam heating. On a radiator in the test room I once dropped a cable coupled directly to some very large cells installed on the flat roof outside; I have forgotten the voltage but the amperage was very large and a large piece of radiator was burnt. I used to get very dirty and fought a losing battle to keep my hands clean; the use of a preparation called Gres-Solvent caused havoc with my skin and it has never recovered.

We used roads through London as a race track

My memory of the early part of 1920 is quite clear; the house at Wimbledon had become vacant and my mother had gone there to prepare to re-let it when I developed a severe abscess. I was obliged to have this removed under a general anaesthetic which was done at Elmside while my mother was there. After this I spent a short period of recuperation at Witney and did not return to Sterndale Road until February.

In the meantime I had bought another motor cycle at Hardwick, this was a two-stroke TDC de luxe for which I paid £19; having walked across the fields to buy it I then pushed it home to Witney. When I got back to London I promptly sold it at a small profit without using it. Early in March, after considering various other machines, I bought for £17 something that had started life as a 1911 Triumph. This was incomplete and the owner had started to modernise it by dropping the frame at the rear of the petrol tank, but from this nucleus I built up a reasonably modern and reliable machine. This necessitated a great deal of work – I made a new petrol tank, a carrier, foot rests and a band brake and provided mudguards, a saddle and panniers etc., I also had the frame stove enamelled. The engine was in very good condition and there was no clutch or gearbox, the drive being direct from a V pulley on the engine to the back wheel by a rubber V belt. Apart from the hours of work I spent doing the work, the total cost to me (including registration and licence £1.5.0 and insurance 15/-) amounted to under £30 and for this I had a motor cycle that was reliable and quite presentable. In fact, I used it for the whole of the summer of 1920, including some trips to Leicester and a great many to Witney. Not once did it fail me. Of course I had minor troubles such as belt slip in wet weather on tarred roads (for this I carried a

An early (c.1910) Triumph motorbike which Barry rebuilt.

46

concoction of powdered resin mixed with rubber solution) and I had a broken brake rod which I mended with wire. It was fast for those days and it was capable of a good performance on any hill likely to be encountered in the area, provided the speed could be maintained. In fact it performed far better than the Douglas owned by Jack Hughes who accompanied me on my expeditions. Of course we had adventures but no serious accidents; I went through the hedge on a bend near Dorchester and I splintered the wing of a trap with my brake lever near Maidenhead. Jack had concussion from a spill at Colnbrook when I was not with him and twice got caught in a speed trap in a 10 mph limit.

Jack Hughes.

Later in the summer we were sometimes joined by Jack Bartlett whose father, Uncle Oswald, had provided him with a small V twin Centaur; this was made by Humber and had a multiple disc clutch in the hub of the back wheel which often gave trouble. We had great enjoyment from our motor cycles and conditions were ideal. Most of the roads were almost empty of traffic and there were few restrictions, we experienced the real joy of the open road although some of the surfaces could be poor by present standards but we were carefree and very lucky.

I had a great affection for the Triumph; its flexibility was amazing for a single speed, fixed-drive machine, it could be started by 'paddling' and was controllable at almost any speed and under any conditions. Can you imagine riding in top gear without a clutch through London or Maidenhead? This was no trouble at all. On one occasion I took my mother on the carrier and on another occasion I took a girl and a large suitcase to Wilcote (where I was entertained with strawberries and cream). It would and did run on a mixture of petrol and paraffin.

Family Motor Cycles

<u>Auto-wheel</u> c.1917.

<u>FN</u> single-cylinder, shaft drive c.1912.

<u>De Dion</u> coil ignition, with the surface carburettor replaced by B & B c.1903.

<u>Triumph</u> single-cylinder, direct belt drive, modernised c.1911.

<u>Douglas</u> 2¾, two-speed, direct belt drive, ex.WD c.1916, purchased February 1921 (cost £38).

<u>FN</u> four-cylinder, two-speed and clutch, shaft drive, electric light c.1913, purchased at Chatham Market 1921 (£38.10.0) seldom ran on four cylinders, I received many shocks from projecting plugs until they were guarded.

<u>Douglas</u> standard 2¾ flat twin, date unknown, the engine was very rough and it blew up in Oxford soon after I sold it in 1921.

<u>Triumph</u> 3½ cylinder, shaft gearbox and clutch, belt drive, ex.WD c.1915, reliable and fast, used for some time and ridden to Devon (on this I spiked an unfortunate sparrow on the brake).

<u>Coulson Blackburn</u> with spring frame with large outside flywheel, one of the best, well-behaved machines I had, docile and lively, c.1921.

<u>Triumph</u> standard 3½ but later than the WD, very sound and reliable (bought at Minster for £50).

<u>Rudge</u> multi-variable gear by expanding belt pulleys, c.1921, fast, reliable and trouble free (on this I rode from Witney to Cirencester and back in little over an hour).

<u>Triumph</u> single-speed c.1912, almost unused when I had it (I seized up the engine at Farmoor with no apparent after-effects).

<u>Scott</u> water-cooled, two-cylinder, two-stroke, fast but very unreliable, c.1914.

<u>American Excelsior</u> large V twin and sidecar, date unknown, could be dangerous when it eventually picked up speed, almost devoid of brakes.

<u>Enfield</u> two-stroke c.1919, very uninteresting.

<u>Morgan</u> three-wheeler, V twin, water-cooled, JAP fast but difficult to control, suffered from transmission troubles, date unknown.

<u>BSA</u> and sidecar, 4 hp, single-cylinder which I used a lot but did not own.

<u>Triumph</u> standard c.1918, which I rode to Devon.

<u>ABC</u> (Sopwith), flat twin across frame, chain drive c.1922, lent to me by J.H.B.

<u>Ner-a-Car</u> two-stroke, slow and uninteresting.

<u>Sunbeam</u> single-cylinder c.1924 which I used quite a lot about 1929 but did not own.

Witney was less than two hours' drive away: I think from door to door I once managed it in 1 hour 25 minutes. If I stopped the night at Twyford, I could be home in an hour in the morning. It was dusty, very dusty, and one could get very, very wet but it was enjoyable and the sun usually shone – or so I now picture it.

Towards the end of the summer I had other things to think about and in September I decided to sell the Triumph. The first person to answer the advertisement bought it for what I asked, £37, and rode it away. Although I had many other motor cycles of all dates and sizes there was never another that gave me the thrill and enjoyment that I got from this first Triumph and I shall always remember it with nostalgia. It was some time before I had another because I was occupied in other ways, on which I will elaborate later, but this may be the appropriate time to provide a list of all the motor cycles that I have used. Most of those that I owned were sold at a small profit and they all provided experience and enjoyment although, at the time, some of the experiences were unwelcome and unpleasant.

After parting with the Triumph, I borrowed Jack Hughes' Douglas, to get to Witney for the Christmas of 1920 and Jack Bartlett came with me as a pillion passenger. It was so cold that we had difficulty in keeping the water in the acetylene generator from freezing and we travelled a lot of the way without lights. The roads were ice covered and the journey was prolonged and unpleasant. Even travelling in summer was not always pleasant, although we usually carried some sort of protective clothing. This was seldom proof against really heavy and continuous rain and, in the early twenties, after six hours of real rain on the journey to Devon I was very wet in spite of several stops. At Nettlebed I once got so wet that I went into a pub and stripped off all my clothes to try to dry out.

Freedom from serious accidents must be attributed to some extent to good fortune because we did some very foolish things. We were young and the roads were clear, in fact almost devoid of traffic as we know it now. I doubt, however, if the speeds we attained were really very high (a speedometer that worked was unusual). I think that the times achieved from one place to another were due more to freedom from obstruction than to speed: there was seldom any need to slow up for anything and we kept going.

We used roads through London as a race track and Joan Theobald, Jack Bartlett and I competed along the stretch from Hammersmith to Holborn, via Cambridge Circus in the evenings to see who could make the best time. When Jack and I went to Bloxham to sell a machine we returned together on another one in less than half an hour to Witney. When riding behind Jack on his ABC I parted company with the carrier at speed over a hump. I took a Triumph to Devon very early one morning in record time to return with Jimmy Hill the same day.

Joan Theobald.

Machines were very crude with few comforts, the first Tan-Sad pillion seat, mounted on springs, was a luxury for the passenger but brakes were very inefficient. It was almost instinctive to find a way through rather than try to stop for an obstruction. Both Jack and I escaped anything serious in the early days and it was not until we were riding more sophisticated machines and had become more careful and sedate (I think) that we both experienced bad accidents and in neither case was speed involved.

Uncle Oswald to the rescue again

From my earliest years I had been attracted by the atmosphere and surroundings during my frequent visits to Witney and later on I was often reminded of this by the contrast with my life in London. During the summer of 1920 this became more and more apparent to me and the idea of living in Witney permanently seemed to offer much of what I valued. I was not unhappy in London and I was still interested in the work I was doing, but the solution appeared to me to lie in finding a job in Witney. I thought that if I could get my Uncle Joe to employ me this would provide the answer. At the time I do not think that building as a career had any particular attraction but I thought it might offer more scope and interest than what I was doing. I was confident that any problems could be overcome once I established myself at Witney.

My Uncle Oswald's reactions were far from enthusiastic – he pointed out, amongst other things, that I had already embarked on a career that offered good prospects and that those at Witney were almost nil. His brother, Joe, was ill and had little or no incentive to expand the business, he was harassed by debts and family commitments and the firm was financially unsound. It was most unlikely that my employment would be of any benefit to them or to me.

My mother, who discussed everything of importance with me very fully, made no attempt to persuade or dissuade me and I decided to proceed with my original intentions. I think that she really approved and it was she who made the first approach to my Uncle Joe. It was some time before he would agree to have me and he made the condition that I should first get experience with another builder. This was not easy as I had nothing to offer. I spent some time trying unsuccessfully to find a firm that would have me and enlisted the help of such people as Thomas Rayson, W. Carmichael of MO Works, Cox of Maidenhead and various builders but it was Uncle Oswald who eventually came to the rescue again. In his early days in London he had a close friend, Jack Theobald, who had now become the senior partner in a firm of quantity surveyors, Gardner & Theobald, in Gower Street. He was approached on my behalf and with his influence, it was agreed that I should be accepted by Courtney & Fairburn Ltd of Albany Road, Camberwell, as a pupil but without any payment on either side. I started there in September 1920.

With the irresponsibility of youth I gave little thought to anything but the immediate future. I had not been earning much before but it had been nearly enough to pay for my rooms. Now, this had to be provided from my mother's slender income and although we had always been careful in spending, now every halfpenny had to be considered still more carefully. At the time, I did not realise how difficult it must have been for my mother to provide for my necessities which were never stinted but, for my part, it taught me the value of money, the abhorrence of waste and the ability to obtain the best value for any payment made. I went

Carrie Taylor.

by train each morning from Hammersmith to Elephant & Castle from where I walked to Albany Road to arrive at 8.00 a.m. Mrs Davie provided me with breakfast early in the morning, I had a frugal lunch at ABC Express or Lyons, costing perhaps a shilling, and a good evening meal was ready when I returned to Sterndale Road. All travelling to sites was by bus or train and these expenses were recoverable but we never cheated.

Courtney & Fairburn's offices were in a double-fronted house in Albany Road. The business had been started by the parents of the present partners, one of whom may have lived there. At the rear, in what had been the garden, was open storage for timber, scaffolding and plant. At the far end was a large building the lower part of which was used for storage. The upper floor was a joinery works. They did not seem to have any mechanical plant or transport; all haulage was hired and horses and carts were used on sites.

They were a medium-sized firm employing about 100 men and the office staff consisted of the two partners, an accountant, an estimator, a wages clerk and a general clerk. There were two supervising surveyors (Holcome and Batley) with whom I spent most of my time. The manufacture of joinery was controlled by a foreman named Reed who ruled the shop and did not welcome any interruption. There was a comprehensive stock of general materials and quite a lot of timber under the control of a yardman-cum-storekeeper and at the end of the year (1920) I was given the task of stocktaking.

I was fortunate in having the opportunity of a fairly comprehensive insight into the administration in the offices and on all the sites that included general contracting, maintenance and repairs. We built a hospital at Isleworth, a bank at Grays, an hotel at Caterham (the Caterham Arms), a large house at Purley, pubs in Little Newport Street and Putney and many private houses. One of my jobs was to convey the wages to sites on pay day, often alone. Although I was entrusted with quite large sums of money, I can remember no precautions being taken against theft and I doubt if any insurance cover existed.

Craftsmen and labourers could earn about £3 and £2 respectively for a week of around 50 hours and time keeping was good. The office staff came in at 8.00 a.m. and worked to 5.00 p.m. but if we were out on a site the time we arrived home depended on trains and buses and work was often taken home to be ready for the morning. There seemed to me some lack of communication between the principals and the staff but my very junior position may have created this impression. Everyone was most helpful to me, particularly Holcome and Batley who went out of their way to instruct me in everything they thought would prove useful to me. Neither could have had much experience in the building industry, they were young and not long demobilised but they were ambitious and made up for their lack of experience by applying a great deal of basic common sense to all they did. They were both very loyal to the firm they worked for and the general atmosphere was good with everyone pulling together.

Not only did they teach me quite a lot of basic technical building construction and administration but they gave me a lot of good advice on the relationship between employer and employee. On the assumption that I might one day become an employer, they endeavoured to ensure that I was aware of some of the pitfalls and ways in which I might be misled. I do not know why they were so helpful to me – in the case of Holcome I think he may have been slightly envious of the opportunities that might result from my connection with a family business – but I cannot speak too highly of all with whom I came in contact during my short period with the firm. In such a short time it was of course impossible for me to touch more than the fringe but I am sure that had I started at Witney without any experience at all it would have been far more difficult for me to attain any position of responsibility and I am grateful to those whose wisdom overruled my impulsive impatience.

The renewal of my uncle's friendship with John Theobold, when he got him to introduce me to Courtney & Fairburn, resulted in the closer association of their two families. I remember picnics in Richmond Park and other outings with Joan Theobald and her step-mother. Joan, Jack Bartlett and I all had motor cycles and spent much time together, and she came to stay at Witney during the summer of 1921. Although I did not see much of John Theobald, he was always helpful to me and many, many years later I renewed the association whilst he was still active in the business.

During the period I spent with Courtney & Fairburn my days were very full and on some evenings I attended classes at the Polytechnic where I met other boys most of whom I have forgotten. Some, however, I regret not having kept in touch with and one named Burch, with whom I was particularly friendly, became well known in Building Federation circles.

Altogether I crowded into this few months a great deal of activity, my main ambition was to get to Witney but I was too busy to feel happy or unhappy in what I was doing then. To those actively engaged in building construction, the winter months are not attractive. They bring all the frustrations caused by rain, snow, frost and mud to most sites but I have no outstanding impressions of this during the winter of 1920/21. Apart from a very cold spell in December, the weather seemed kind. My greatest impressions are of travelling – the cold dark mornings and long cold bus journeys – I sold my Swift cycle and I never used a cycle or motor cycle while I was there. All movement was by bus or train or on foot and the time spent in this way accounted for a great deal of the day. The day might start with the early train journey and walk to the office by 8.00 a.m. and later there was a journey to Fenchurch Street Station to get a train to Grays via Dagenham and Rainham, perhaps visiting a job at Plaistow or Ilford.

Grays Station, which was quite small, adjoined the level crossing and industry had not yet reached Dagenham. The surrounding country was flat and marshy. A few yards up the High Street at Grays was the bank we were building and next door was a café run by an Italian who provided coffee. I was shown the party wall which was in danger of collapsing; it had been built of 4½ inch stocks in mortar, without any ties whatsoever, to a height of three storeys. Although I have no clear memory of the train journeys to Caterham, I remember thawing out in a café in Croydon after a bus ride from Purley and later proceeding by a petrol-electric Tilling-Stevens to get home late at night. No doubt our forebears would have welcomed anything faster and warmer than a horse and trap but the open top of a bus could be very cold.

Local jobs like Putney, Little Newport Street or the Cock Tavern were quite easily accessible and at the latter I spent quite a lot of time and looked on it as 'my job'. The kitchens were in the basement approached by a circular iron stairs and the walls were thick with grease. We did a lot to bring the drainage more up to date with cast iron concealed gulleys and new drains. Fire precautions consisted of teak doors throughout the building with glazing bedded in wash-leather strips. I remember being impressed by the speed of bricklaying at Isleworth but the Little Newport Street site was very cramped, we had to climb up to the foreman's office and it was difficult to get steelwork into position because the licensed bar had to be kept open. Here was my first experience of hot asphalting. We were also carrying out some work at a bank in Cambridge Circus and, for some reason, I made several visits to a firm called Art Pavements & Decorations at Finsbury Circus, probably connected with tiling. Altogether I was kept quite busy and I had the opportunity to absorb quite a lot of useful information.

I was still interested in motorcycles and I bought a Douglas ex War Office (WO) machine for £38 in February 1921 which I soon sold at a small profit and then bought a four-cylinder FN from a doctor at Chatham for £38.10.0; it was of 1914 vintage but had a gearbox, clutch, electric light etc. and I kept it for some time. The facilities at Kensington were no longer available to me so I rented a shed near Sterndale Road adjoining Brook Green where I could keep the machine and I remember how cold it was there. I missed the workshop that I had been able to use when I was at Kensington Court but I still spent a lot of time at Aynhoe Road and my Uncle Oswald was always available with help and advice. In fact, I was just as much a member of the family and took part in most of their activities and outings, particularly at weekends.

I remember trips to the Hog's Back with tea at Guildford – the Portsmouth road – Richmond Park and Richmond with the famous 'Maids of Honour' and many other outings, which we enjoyed, often accompanied by other friends in other cars or motor cycles. The Theobolds had a small 10 hp Singer which I sometimes drove. It once broke down at the Piccadilly end of Regent Street where we left it, while we went by bus to return later with a rope and another car to tow it home.

Aynhoe Road was a meeting place where everyone seemed welcome and my aunt and uncle had many friends. Jack Hughes was a frequent visitor in the evenings and there was Williams, who helped me so much at the Court, the Theobalds and Squires, who was the Resident Engineer at Chelsea. He had a car suspended on compressed air cylinders; many years later I met him again when he had retired to Bognor.

Harry Noakes, who had been a great friend of my father, lived in a flat in Aynhoe Road almost opposite No. 40 and I often met him at the swimming baths in Lime Grove. I spent a lot of time at these baths, though they did not provide the very high diving facilities that were available to me at Wimbledon, but they were only a few minutes' cycle ride from Sterndale Road and I enjoyed myself there, sometimes going twice a day.

Among the visitors to Aynhoe Road I remember a Miss Partridge who lived at Ealing and who still used a small tub drawn by a pony which she tied to a tree on the edge of the pavement outside the house.

From the time when I first lived at Aynhoe Road in 1918, I remember with gratitude Auntie Maud who did so much to make me welcome; the background of her efficient organisation made life very pleasant. There was never any fuss but she was always there to smooth things out, probably I knew her better than anyone outside her own family because I lived as part of it. I learned a lot from her strong character and optimism. It was after I had left London that Auntie Maud and Uncle Oswald moved from Aynhoe Road to Luxembourg Gardens. This road was on the opposite side of Brook Green and the house overlooked Bute House gardens. It was a similar house but somewhat larger and the front room on the ground floor had been made into a garage which held two cars. Above this, on the first floor was a large sitting room the full width of the house. For some years after I left London, I would arrive and take it for granted

Shoreham 1919 – Maud Joslin, Jack, Oswald with Molly and Maud Bartlett.

50

that I would be put up for the night and I often slept on the floor in this room. Auntie Maud came to visit us in Witney after I married and when Uncle Oswald retired, in about 1938, they bought a house in Brize Norton; I then saw a lot of both of them. Later they moved to Abinger Hammer where she died in 1946.

When I lived in London, both Jack and Molly were very much part of my life and my association with Jack continued for some years after he left the brewery at Mortlake. In the early days of his car dealing, when he had premises in Warren Street and later in Westbourne Grove, I frequently visited him and bought a number of cars from him. Molly and I never hit it off very well in the earlier years, and there was quite a difference in our ages. It was not until many years later and after she married, that I really appreciated her character.

Even fogs had some promise of adventure

As the time that I spent with Courtney & Fairburn drew to a close I was eagerly looking forward to when I should be able to live at Witney and although I was then anxious to get away, I can now look back on the few years that I spent in London with a certain amount of nostalgia. Allowing for the lapse of time and a memory that I am beginning to mistrust I will try to paint some sort of mental picture of that part of London with which I was familiar in those days.

First of all, there was very little traffic, and not much noise. Side streets and those in residential areas, were almost deserted at times, children could and did play there. Even in main roads and areas such as Hammersmith Broadway and Shepherds Bush there was no congestion or hold up, nor any difficulty in walking or cycling in the road. Pedestrian crossings and traffic lights had not been thought of. Where trams ran – Goldhawk Road, Uxbridge Road, Fulham Palace Road, King Street etc. – they ran in the middle of the road and all other traffic kept to the left of them which caused a few delays where the trams stopped, as other traffic had to give way to the tram passengers getting on or off. Where the tramlines ended, approaching Hammersmith or at the Bayswater end of Shepherds Bush, there were usually a bunch of trams waiting their turn and having feeder arms reversed and destinations changed.

Most of the surfaces were of wood blocks which became very slippery but this was common to other roads and I remember using the very wide roads at Kensington, such as Exhibition Road, which were all wood block surfaces and almost devoid of any traffic, for the purpose of practising controlled skidding. Those who were fortunate enough to have the use of a car or motorcycle parked where they wished to stop and no one objected if they were left all day (or night provided they were lit). Little and no precaution was taken against theft and I frequently left a cycle or motorcycle for long periods in Sterndale Road, Aynhoe Road or outside the baths in Lime Grove. Most people were honest; assault, mugging or smash and grab were unheard of in fact, you went where you wished and walked about without fear in daytime or at night.

Brook Green itself was often almost deserted and the bell of the convent rang without any competition. The surrounding roads, like others in the area, were disturbed only by an occasional coal cart, milk float, rag and bone cart or other horse-drawn vehicle together with a few boys with cycles equipped with frames for baskets or with boxes on three wheels pedalled from the rear; the original AC delivery vehicle described earlier was based on these and Auto Carriers later produced cars at Thames Ditton under S. F. Edge.

Blythe Road, which ran rather tortuously between Shepherds Bush Road and Hammersmith Road, was a convenient shopping centre. Aynhoe Road ran directly between it and Brook Green. At one end was the elite residential Brook Green and at the other a pub on the corner that might be termed a gin palace with its bottle and jug entrance in Aynhoe Road. A little lower down Blythe Road, next to a large laundry, Sterndale Road commenced. It curved abruptly towards Shepherds Bush Road and lower down were access roads to both Brook Green and Blythe Road. In the latter, at the Shepherds Bush Road end, were all sorts of trade premises such as small builders' stores with long ladders standing upright, Kosher meat suppliers, various small workshops and livery stables where quite a lot of horses were stabled. Beyond the laundry by Sterndale Road, the shopping area started and beyond Aynhoe Road and a few shops, was the Post Office Savings Bank building. This was the head office and was set in extensive grounds with gardens and recreational facilities including some hard tennis courts: Harry Noakes, who held a position of some importance in the Savings Bank, lived close by in the flats in Aynhoe Road. I remember watching him play tennis on the red hard courts.

A little beyond and adjoining these grounds was the General Post Office in Blythe Road and further on were more shops as far as the junction of Blythe Road with the main Hammersmith Road at the side of Olympia. Instead of following this road past the Post Office to the main road, a quicker way to Kensington was to turn left into a short road that led to the railway side of Olympia. This ended in a barrier of posts beyond which was the pedestrian precinct outside the entrance to Olympia and from this, on the left, was the entrance to Addison Road Station. There was no difficulty in walking or cycling through this area on the way towards Addison Bridge and I habitually cycled this way to Kensington. In fact I became so confident of negotiating the posts that I did this with 'no hands' – until I came to grief at speed by tipping a post with the handlebars.

After Addison Bridge most of the road to Kensington was residential as far as Earls Court Road where Strachan & Brown, the coachbuilders, had premises on the corner. After Earls Court Road, shops were continuous on the north side, amongst these was a landmark in the shape of a large clock projecting over the wide pavement and here was Lorbergs, a shop with a fascinating display of such things as model boats, engines, clocks, watches, sports equipment and toys. Here I made my first purchase when I arrived in January 1918, a clock watch with a dial that could be read in the dark. It cost 6/- and gave me many years of noisy but trouble-free service.

Beyond Lorbergs was the Kensington that I knew so well with the premises of Hornes, Pontings, Barkers, Derry & Toms before reaching Kensington Court turn, opposite which was the Palace Hotel, the fire station and Slatters, then Church Street and St. Mary Abbots Church. The entrance to Kensington Court from the High Street was a narrow cul-de-sac providing vehicular access to the generating station and also to a paved pedestrian area bounded by a row of posts between this and the roadway of the residential part of the Court; inside the station at Kensington Court all was noise and activity but the Court itself was a quiet area where children played and vehicles were almost unknown. Colonel Compton, who founded the firm of Compton Parkinson, was an eccentric character frequently to be seen walking from his house to the offices which were opposite the generating station.

Fogs, known as pea soupers, were frequent in those days and during the war there were no lights which made any impression on them – visibility was really nil and one groped along buildings or the kerb and took off into the unknown when crossing a road. I remember leaving the entrance to the Blythe Road Post Office in one of these and being asked, while standing on the step, to direct someone to the Post Office.

Hammersmith and Shepherds Bush were my happy hunting grounds where I spent a great deal of my time in the evenings; each lay only a short walk from Sterndale Road. Hammersmith Broadway was approached by crossing Brook Green and turning left opposite the Osram lamp factory into the main road a few hundred yards along which was the Broadway. Shepherds Bush Green was in the opposite direction turning right from Blythe Road and it was about the same distance to Goldhawk Road. At the Hammersmith Broadway were five main roads; clockwise from Shepherds Bush Road was the highway to Kensington, then Fulham Palace Road, then the Barnes Road over the river bridge, then King Street leading to Chiswick and finally the road where the trams were diverted to the depot and which led back into King Street. In the Broadway itself were the two stations, a cinema which I frequented and a Palais de Dance in which I took no interest. The Kensington Road passed the other end of Brook Green and on the way lay the hospital, the theatre (where a seat in the gallery cost sixpence), Rowton House and blocks of shops amongst which was a small garage where I was told the first Lagonda car was made by a man named Blackwell. Further on was St. Paul's School and grounds and at the junctions of North End Road and Blythe Road were more shops as far as Addison Road Bridge. Fulham Palace Road had tramlines all the way to Putney and over the bridge, through Putney. Up the hill lay Putney Heath leading to Wimbledon Common. This was the way I sometimes cycled to Wimbledon. The next road over the river bridge I also used to get to Wimbledon through Barnes and Roehampton and on the river below Hammersmith Bridge boats could be hired. Here I occasionally rowed on a skiff and tried out an outrigger with a sliding seat in which I never acquired much skill. It is surprising that I never capsized. King Street and the adjoining area as far as Chiswick were full of interest and I explored them with great enthusiasm in the hope of finding some bargain; a great deal of time was spent at a shop that sold photographic equipment. The area around Shepherds Bush was also combed very thoroughly. Between Goldhawk Road and Uxbridge Road was a connecting road parallel to the railway known as the Arches where endlessly fascinating shops were formed by filling the fronts of the railway arches. On the far side of the railway was Lime Grove and the swimming baths which I used a lot and I spent many happy hours exploring the whole of the area and its surroundings.

These are my memories and impressions of the small corners of London that I knew so well. Although my stay was comparatively short (January 1918 to March 1921), I was at an impressionable age and it seems now to have covered a large slice of my life. When I look back after so long I feel some sense of nostalgia for the experiences I had while I was there, but during the last six months I had some insight into another part of London which I had no regrets about leaving. When I was with Courtney & Fairburn their offices and stores were in Albany Road which is in the area of Newington, Walworth Road and Camberwell Road and the whole of this part seemed to me to be depressing and down at heel. The offices in Albany Road had once been a private dwelling but now the building was gloomy and dirty and it was overlooked by a tall block of flats which added nothing to the outlook. When I said goodbye to all this in May 1921 I was looking forward to going to Witney and I left it all without any regret but I had been fortunate in having made friends with several of the staff and I remember going into a pub near the Elephant & Castle, consuming my first beer and saying goodbye to Holcome, Batley and others who had all been very good to me. While I was in London there were many sunny days, I was young and interested in all I saw and even fogs held some promise of adventure but I was lonely because I never made friends easily and probably this was the prime reason for the attraction that Witney held for me. There I experienced a friendly atmosphere and association with my relations, particularly my grandparents. This made a deep impression on me. I looked on Witney as my home and my one ambition was to live there – the practical problem of being able to earn a living took second place. As things turned out though, the decision to do so was a very wise one and in retrospect it would appear providential.

'Three Musketeers' – Jack, Denis and Barry.

Part Three
MUD ON THE BOOTS

I duly presented myself at the office

My arrival in Witney was uneventful and coincided with the start of the Easter holidays. On Good Friday, I travelled on an FA motorcycle in convoy with my Uncle Oswald in his Adler car. This suffered from a leak which necessitated my scouting ahead for possible supplies of water. Most of my belongings had been sent by rail in a large tool chest and I carried the remainder in a wooden box attached to the carrier.

It had been agreed that I should start work in the office at 75 High Street on the 1st April 1921 which was the following Friday, when I duly presented myself at the office at eight o'clock in the morning. There had been a white frost overnight and the morning was cold but the office was unheated. I was given the task of indexing the letter book which was the usual type of bound flimsy paper on which letters written with copying ink were pressed on a damp backing. Had I realised it at the time, this could have been an excellent opportunity for me to acquire knowledge of the current happenings in the firm, but to me then it was only a chore. If I had troubled to read them at all, they would have meant little to me.

The staff consisted of de Vinny, the manager, and Cousins, the clerk. The former had started the previous April at a salary of £5 a week and had come from South London. He was married with a son and daughter and lodged with Miss Harwood in Bridge Street. Obviously he had had experience in the building trade, but looking back, I think his knowledge was limited to small works. I liked him, he was always very helpful to me and we spent a lot of time together. Cousins came from Cheltenham where he had been employed as a telegraph clerk; he had answered de Vinny's advertisement for a clerk in a builder's office and had started work the previous August at about £2 a week. He too lodged in Witney at a cottage in Mill Street occupied by the Dix family. He was not quite my age, having been born in 1903.

The office, facing up the yard, was well lit with a part glass roof. There was a long sloping desk the whole length of the window and we sat on stools facing the window. There was a door opening directly into the gateway and another small door opposite leading into the house. Between and facing the outer door, de Vinny occupied a large roll-top desk. The office was draughty and only on rare occasions do I remember the small Tortoise stove being lit. I do not remember being unduly cold, everyone accepted it as normal; few houses or offices had much heating and it was almost unheard of in workshops unless the fire was required for a purpose such as heating glue, metal pots or a forge. There was electric lighting in the office and I recall that the brass covers of the switches provided a mild electric shock in damp weather. The wiring was in wood capping, as was that in the adjoining house which was occupied by my Uncle Joe who used a room at the front of the house as an office; this had been used by my Great Uncle Christopher until his death in 1918.

There was no typewriter or telephone on the premises and the equipment in the office consisted of many drawers, a letter press, a few files and drawing equipment. There was a large double-door safe built into the wall and the books, all leather bound, were locked in this at night. It was a pleasant office in the summer, cool for most of the day with the west sun in the evening. All those who came and went through the entrance gateway could be observed, materials and plant booked in or out and most of the yard itself could be seen from the window.

De Vinny had negotiated a contract to build some fifty houses (Highworth Place) in the Crofts for the Urban District Council at a figure of about £1,000 per house and these were well on the way when I arrived. They were constructed of 9 inch solid brick walls, wire cuts obtained from Chawley, were roughcast externally and roofed with red sand-faced tiles on battens without any under-felt. The architect was Thos. Rayson and the quantity surveyor G.T. Gardner, both of Oxford. The contract included the road and sewers; a few of the houses were built by Barnes at a negotiated price. The foreman was Bert Buckingham from Hailey, with a foreman carpenter named Will Smith from Newland. Ellis Griffin of Stonesfield did the plastering which was all on wood laths. In April 1921 the total weekly wages amounted to about £175 paying about fifty men; de Vinny had £6, Cousins about £2.5.0 and probably I had about the same.

There were a few other jobs running mainly, I think, involving alterations or repairs and I recall being sent to the mill at Minster to measure a room in the house for panelling. This corn mill, owned and worked by Tom Jeffries, was still driven by water-power. There were a number of small jobs in or near the town and I went on my motorcycle to visit work at Asthall Vicarage, Ramsden Vicarage and two jobs at Kencot.

In the yard, there was virtually no transport; a two-cylinder Adler car of about 1909 vintage was out of use and there was a single-cylinder de Dion that was even older, also unusable. There was a decrepit grey horse that was almost too old to work and at one time there had been a pony, used long ago by my uncle's wife, Nancy. The use of two-wheeled trucks was extensive, labour was cheap and a pushing-truck cost less than other forms of transport. The movement of plant and materials outside the immediate precincts of the town was achieved by hiring. Some of the stores and workshops in the yard were inconvenient and outdated but basically the layout had been well thought out and was still very sound.

This then is a brief outline of the conditions that existed when I came to Witney in 1921. It must be borne in mind that what had at one time been a very flourishing business had suffered blow after blow and had drifted on to the verge of bankruptcy. The prosperity that Bartlett Brothers had achieved by around 1875 had been marred by a very heavy loss sustained on a large contract at Freeland. They appear, however, to have recovered from this and in early 1900 they were doing a considerable volume of work controlled by the original partners Christopher and Joseph together with Joseph junior, my uncle.

The first blow came in 1908 when my uncle lost his wife, Nancy, and baby son, a tragedy from which he never appeared to recover. Then in 1910 his father, Joseph, died at the age of 69. Christopher, who had for many years suffered the results of a form of polio, was an invalid and unable to leave the office and had become very set in his ways. In 1912 Joe had a serious motor accident near Woodstock whilst driving the Adler car. He was so badly smashed up that it is surprising that he lived; the effects of his injuries remained all his life. One can imagine the effect that all this had on the conduct of the business. It is surprising that it survived and a credit to the tenacity of Christopher and others in the family who rallied to its aid. It is also surprising that my uncle recovered sufficiently to carry out one or two quite sizeable contracts prior to 1914 and to keep going, almost single-handed, during the war years when at one time the wage roll was down to eleven men. There was little incentive for him to modernise or expand when it was over, but his choice of de Vinny as manager was, I think, quite sound.

Their temperaments were very different and this very soon led to friction that affected their relationship. De Vinny was full of enthusiasm, anxious to cut corners and make more money whereas my uncle was cautious, conservative and reluctant to alter the tried old ways which had resulted in the quality of workmanship of which so many examples survive. With hindsight, one can see both of their viewpoints but I am inclined to believe that there was a great deal of wisdom in my uncle's outlook. On the other hand de Vinny was an extrovert whose personality was a great asset in obtaining work and one is tempted to imagine what could have been the result if there had been a harmonious relationship between the two. However it is idle to speculate on the rights and wrongs of their individual outlooks and presumptuous to imagine that my arrival had the slightest effect on their views. In fact, I was so wrapped up in my own affairs that I paid little attention to the conduct of the business. In those early days, I missed the guiding hand of my Uncle Oswald.

I dreamed dreams about transport

I was involved with things mechanical, motorcycles and cars and the one thing that I did achieve was some improvement in transport. I had my motorcycle but others were not so mobile until I persuaded my uncle to buy a car. This was an early Wolseley, found in London by Uncle Oswald, and had been modernised with a two-seater body; I drove it for many miles. It had one persistent fault, a clutch which either gummed up or slipped and needed constant attention. Later on, I got the old Adler going and sold it. The de Dion was also disposed of.

At this time in Witney, there were two rival firms who ran lorries for hire, Harry Haines who had been a driver at Smith's mill and the Witney Transport Company run by Wigglesworth and King. Haines pinned his faith in chain-drive Albions and used nothing else – quite successfully. The other firms, of which more anon, used an assortment of vehicles. King was a plausible fellow and through him we bought a small Napier van from Slough. It cost £150 and when the top was removed it made quite a presentable lorry to carry about 25 cwt. It had solid tyres, the footbrake operated on the transmission shaft and the hand brake on expanded shoes in drums on the back wheels; these rang like bells so that it could be heard a long way off. Eventually we quietened this by clamping strip lead around them. On anything but a dry road, it had a habit of proceeding crabwise at the slightest use of the brake and it was not very good either up or down hills. It was driven by Charles Monk who was engaged as a driver/mechanic in 1921; he stayed with the firm for nearly fifty years. Latterly he became a storekeeper but he looked after my own car for me, without a break, until 1974. Before 1921, he had driven the Royal Mail van in the very early days of motor transport and had been wounded in the 1914–18 war.

Charles Monk with the small Napier van. With the top removed it was transformed into a 'presentable lorry'.

Of course, I dreamed dreams about transport and imagined that one day I might be in control of gleaming Thornycroft or Leyland lorries in the yard. A little later on we did acquire a Model T Ford van! This did a vast amount of work over several years. It was overloaded and abused but never really let us down. Like so many others, this had a left-hand driving position. The back doors were removed and long lengths of timber could be carried each side of the cab, with other materials in the bed. It was usually driven by Jethro Collins, but I also used it for many journeys. I recall the lights that almost went out when the speed dropped (there was no battery) …. grinding up the long hills from Moreton at night loaded with men and cycles and an aching foot from holding low gear for so long …. watching the rear wheel roll on in front after breaking a half-shaft at Barton …. tearing off a front cover at Fordwells by cornering too fast and driving through floods, with the bed awash, at Cannon Pool. I remember too the quick steering and the lively engine. This was rated at about 15 hp and was heavy to swing, in fact the drag of the epicyclic gears on cold mornings made it so difficult that one back wheel was always jacked up. The standard chassis of this model could be converted by fitting sprockets to the half-shafts and driving, by chains, wheels on another axle which carried an extension of the chassis, so that a bed carrying 30 cwt or more could be fitted. For a short time, we had one of these but it was not a success because it was secondhand and already worn out by Witney Transport Company!

When I first arrived, the old coach-house accommodated one car whilst petrol was kept in a small brick store on the far side of the field. This held a 40 gallon drum that was rolled in from the side so that the fuel could be drawn into circular cans supplied by Carless, Capel & Leonard.

Next to the lime kiln was an open Dutch barn which we made into a roomy garage by closing the end and forming a front with two pairs of large doors. It was floored with concrete slabs and provided ample space for three vehicles, together with a bench and workshop space. Water was obtained from a large rain-water tank on piers and later a small petrol pump was installed outside. By this time, my Uncle Percy had a van or vans and the installation provided petrol at a cheaper rate for both businesses.

In the early 1920s, this garage was very much part of my life. I spent much of my time there and we did nearly all the repairs and maintenance of the vehicles we had, albeit very crudely for there was little equipment. However it extended to fitting big-ends and new pistons and as I acquired cars, I did a lot of work on these, entirely rebuilding two from the bare chassis.

I frequently travelled about with de Vinny and my uncle because I nearly always drove them. The experience of witnessing their activities must have rubbed off on me even though I regarded this job as a chore that hindered me. Looking back, I feel that my uncle was very patient because at times my outlook must have seemed very strange to him. Only once do I remember any definite rebuke when he said "If you spent as much time and paid as much attention to what you do here as you do to your own amusements, it would be better for the business in which I hope one day you will have a share". At the time this made little impression on me, but I continue to remember it.

The Ford with Charles Monk c.1934.

55

Grandmother Jessie Bartlett.

My grandmother expressed strong disapproval

I lived at 71 High Street in my grandmother's house with my mother until 1929. When I arrived in 1921, this seemed to offer the acme of comfort by the standards then prevailing. In the kitchen there was a large Eagle range on which everything was cooked but there was no other heating except coal fires. In the scullery there was a large stone sink and by this a hand pump that could also be used to pump water to a tank which flushed the WC upstairs. This pump drew water from a well fed by a deep borehole situated between my grandmother's house and that of my uncle and used by both houses. It was beautiful clear spring water but very hard, however there was a plentiful supply of soft water from rainwater tanks. Adjoining the woodshed was a large wash-house with a large copper and enormous mangle, in the base of which was a type of washing machine. Next to the wash-house was the closet with two seats over a vault and beyond this a brick ash bin. All of these were shaded by a large yew tree and screened by ivy.

The whole of the house and outbuildings were covered in Virginia creeper, which was brilliant red in the autumn. There was a greenhouse heated by a coke boiler, this and the garden were looked after by Forester. He and Fred Busby had started work as carters in 1881 and had remained in the employment of Bartlett Brothers since that date. For some time, Forester had tended the gardens, fed the stock and generally supported both families.

By choice I slept in the attic of 71 High Street which gave me the advantage of an adjoining room where I had a hip-bath, however all the water had to be carted up and down the stairs. In winter the room was at times so cold that ice formed but I was quite content; hot water was provided, each morning, by the maid and my shoes were cleaned by Forester. This was luxury.

I am quite sure that at times my presence must have jarred on the senses of my grandmother in her declining years but at the time I was oblivious of this. My outlook was that of youth and I took for granted that change was good. Perhaps it was, but some of the things that I did must have been disturbing to her and I can only express admiration for her forbearance.

In the early days of wireless my enthusiasm knew no bounds. Not only did I take over the old office adjoining the scullery as a workshop, but I used her drawing room (where I had fixed up an aerial lead) for all kinds of experiments; there were batteries on the floor with components and other equipment all over the furniture. This and other liberties brought little comment but my grandmother expressed strong disapproval when I played tennis on Sunday and again when I invited de Vinny into her sitting room after she had retired; there were a number of old unpaid accounts and he was trying to get them cleared up. I cannot imagine what help I could have been but no doubt we thought that this room was more comfortable than the office at night. I recall thinking her objections were unjust but now can sympathise with her. I am sure there were other things that I took for granted such as providing myself with an electricity supply in my bedroom by removing the wood capping from the supply in the room below and sticking pins through the insulation wires. Looking back, although I feel I sometimes abused the privileges, my life at 71 with my mother and grandmother was extremely happy.

During the summer of 1921, although I spent much time with the vehicles, I was aware of other activities going on. The Crofts contract was drawing to a close, other work was being undertaken and tenders were prepared for local housing schemes as far afield as

Jessie Bartlett at the back of 71 High Street.

Stokenchurch and Northleach. Contracts for a bank in Faringdon, alterations at Coxwell, several farms at Long Wittenham, additions to buildings at Blockley, work at Showell Farm, Shilton and Witney Grammar School were all in progress by early 1922. There were small works for the Bells and Dr Pilkington at Kencot, repairs at Caswell, Minster, Asthall, Ramsden, Alvescot, Hailey, South Leigh and Bampton, as well as in the town and the mills.

The Crofts contract had proved quite profitable and de Vinny had persuaded my uncle to build some houses in the Close, at the rear of the yard with a frontage to Gloucester Place. The first pair were built in stone whilst the others had stone fronts but 9 inch brick was used above joist level on the remaining walls. At this time the building of houses to let was a sound investment which was encouraged by the payment of a subsidy; there was some haste to finish the last of the six before the subsidy was withdrawn. I think the total cost was less than £2000 for the three pairs. The construction was traditional 18 inch walling in lime mortar, wood lintels, a fireplace in every room, lime plastering on sawn laths and roof of clay tiles without under-felt. Good lime came from Breakspears at Northleigh. Almost the first job on a site was for a labourer to dig a lime pit. The lime was slaked in a cauldron covered with a sack then run through a fine sieve into the pit where the resulting putty was left to mature. Cow hair was added to the rendering coat and the toughest mortar was made from road dirt which was obtained by screening the deposit from the side of any local stone road. Fat mortar contained neither cement nor sand but cow dung was added for pargeting flues.

When the Close houses were being built I soon found that I could access 71 via the garden without using the front door which was useful when I was out late. Late one dark night I trod in the lime pit and fell into a pile of mortar. To anyone who knows the properties of lime putty or mortar the result needs little imagination.

Around this time there was great activity in connection with the old war-time aerodrome on the Burford Road. This had become disused after the war and the temporary hangars, which were formed of timber frames and trussed spans covered with canvas, had been sold by auction. They were bought by my uncle and although the covering had been torn to shreds, a large quantity of very sound timber and fittings was salvaged. Now the remaining buildings were about to be offered for sale and it was the policy of the Ministry to clear the sites and return them to the freeholders. At Witney, there were two main areas fronting on to the Burford Road which both had a return frontage on to the road to Curbridge covering about 26 acres in all. Brick buildings had been erected here, ranging from hangars to lavatory blocks, with a complete drainage system and with water mains fed from the Witney water tower.

At the sale, the two large double hangars were bought by Hollands and all the cast iron water mains and manhole covers were purchased by Potters; both firms were based in Thame. My uncle bought or later acquired all the rest of the buildings except a few lots that were taken away. I imagine that a condition of purchase was that the site should be cleared to ground level which meant that the concrete floors were retained and the manholes left uncovered; no doubt this would be taken into account in the compensation paid to the freeholders.

After some prolonged negotiations, the whole of the freehold of the two areas, together with the area of the outfall works lying to the west, were purchased, from the executors of Gallaway, at a cost which worked out at about £25 per acre; there was also an additional parcel of land, that was copyhold, adjoining the road to Curbridge which was purchased later. All this left my uncle in possession of a complete estate on freehold land on the outskirts of Witney, with a sewage system almost in working order. There was no longer any mains water but the site provided an opportunity for development

The hangars at Witney Aerodrome c.1920.

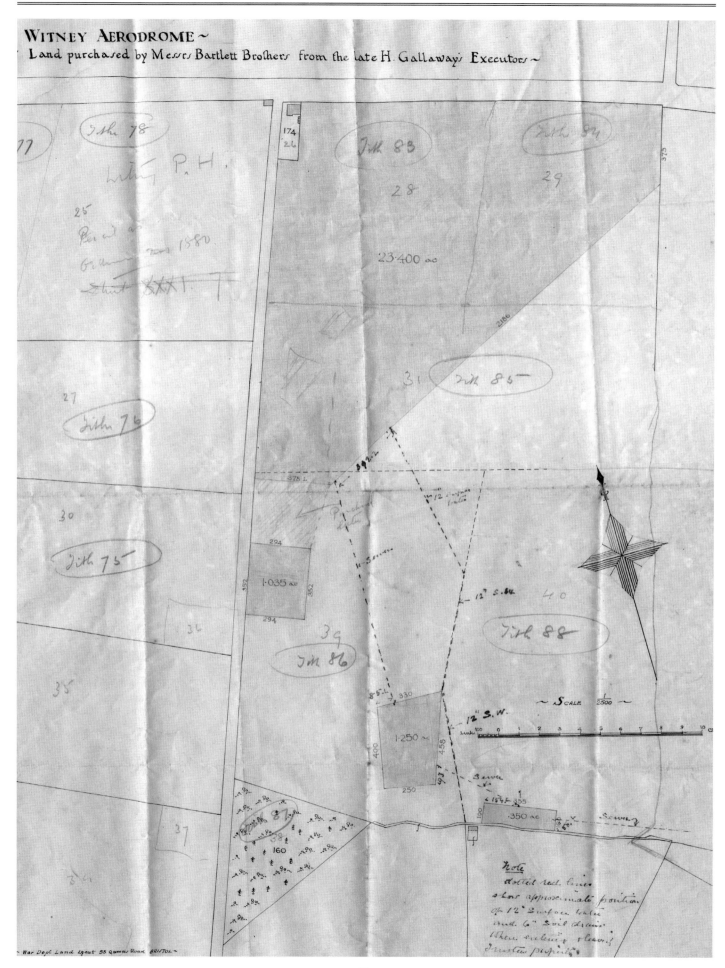

WITNEY AERODROME ~
Land purchased by Messrs Bartlett Brothers from the late H. Gallaway's Executors ~

~ War Dept. Land Agent 33 Queens Road BRISTOL ~

58

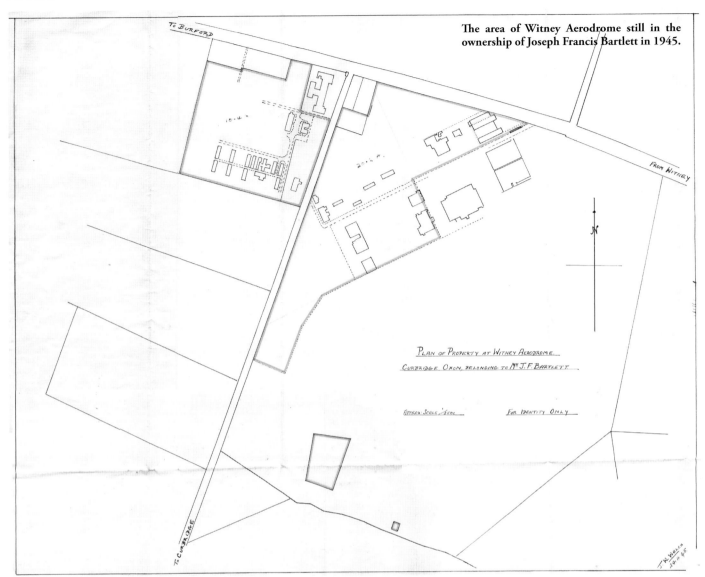

TO BURFORD

FROM WITNEY

N

PLAN OF PROPERTY AT WITNEY AERODROME. CURBRIDGE. OXON, BELONGING TO Mr. J. F. BARTLETT.

APPROX SCALE 1:2500   FOR IDENTITY ONLY

TO CURBRIDGE

J. W. WELCH 24.11.45

which could easily have been financed to provide an enormous appreciation on the outlay. However, it was dealt with piecemeal mainly, I think, because capital was not available.

Some of the buildings were crudely converted into dwellings with wells dug to provide water and some were sold as they stood, including the freehold. C. D. Batt paid £150 for the complete single hangar which he used for playing indoor tennis. The regimental block was purchased by Studts the amusement contractors to store their fairground equipment and Rawlings bought the mess block to use as a garage. All these sales were at what was then considered a fair price and showed a good profit but with hindsight it was a missed opportunity to retain an area of land that was to become more and more valuable. In my lifetime, it became the home of Smiths of England's industrial development. Even after my uncle's death in 1946 no one was far-sighted enough to realise the land's potential and I was instrumental in negotiating the sale of ten acres west of Curbridge Road.

Returning to the 1920s, included in my uncle's purchase were two asphalt hard tennis courts, which I had resurfaced and with the help of Arthur Busby in the evenings, erected stop-netting. The tennis club that I formed to play on them had about twenty players; I believe the subscription was about 15/- a season which about paid expenses. It was a successful venture that provided a great deal of enjoyment.

A Mrs Webb made the teas in the Downs Farm house and I was involved in a pleasant social atmosphere throughout the summer. Some of us also had an open invitation to play each week at Station Farm, South Leigh which was occupied by Charles Bryan, known to us as 'Uncle'; his niece, Nancy Penson, and her mother kept house for him. There was a good grass court, unlimited hospitality with drinks and often home-cured ham for supper.

I sold a gun to buy an engagement ring

Soon after I came to Witney, I met my future wife Mary Tanner and we became part of a large social circle engaged in many activities. When we were unable to play tennis, there was badminton in the YMCA hut. This was really quite unsuitable for the purpose because of its low roof. We danced there, at the Corn Exchange where the highlight was the Red Cross Ball, at Oxford, at Woodstock, at Burford and at some private functions of which Caswell and Yew Tree Farm were outstanding. There were crayfishing parties with picnics by the river at Minster, parties on the river at Rushey Lock, skating on the lake at Eynsham Hall by moonlight and tobogganing when there was snow. We were surrounded by a great number of friends of whom alas so very few now remain. I was naturally shy and retiring but it was Mary's influence and help that enabled me to take part in these enjoyments.

Mary Tanner, later to be Mary Taylor.

Barry and Mary at Witney Aerodrome tennis court.

Cray fishing parties at the River Windrush: standing, left to right – Dick Bartlett. Barry Taylor, Jack Bartlett, Jimmy Hill and below Denis Bartlett, right – unknown.

Picnics by the river: Left to right – Mary Tanner, Dick Bartlett, Jessie Wheeler, Jimmy Hill, Jessie Bartlett, Jack Bartlett, Maud Joslin, unknown and Denis Bartlett.

At Rushey, Barry at the rear with Mary to the right.

Tobogganing at Northleigh, Barry is on the right.

ODGREEN. WITNEY.   AA58

To the right of centre, The Chestnuts, Woodgreen, Witney pictured c.1940.

From our first meeting, she was my constant inspiration. For over fifty years, it was her influence that guided me and inspired me in all my ambitions, in both business and in my social life.

In the early twenties, the Chestnuts on Woodgreen, where Mary's parents lived, became a second home to me and I learned a great deal from the people I met there. I got on well with her parents. Her father had retired in 1918 from active participation in an engineering business in London and had come to live at the Chestnuts. He still had an interest in the business that he and his late brother had started in Camden Town which later, was carried on by his two sons Selby and Bert; at one time they had made ocean-going steam tugs which they launched onto the canal. They were steeped in engineering law and I was very interested in the type of work that they carried out. We all talked the same language.

Mrs Tanner came from Jersey where her family had many connections with shipping and the sea. Not only was she very kind to me but I always felt that I could talk to her. She gave me advice on etiquette, entertaining, the use of wine and liqueurs and similar subjects. Although at the time I had no particular interest, I found later this knowledge to be an asset. Mr Tanner's elder brother, Sir Henry Tanner, was well known as an architect and had been knighted for his services to the Crown during the period when he held the appointment as Chief Architect with HM Office of Works.

I was very fortunate that, at the Chestnuts, there were so many opportunities for me to meet a great many people of substance in the worlds of building, architecture and engineering.

My interest in cars was always very much to the fore and the ones that I drove were many and varied. In the paddock beyond the garden at the Chestnuts, was a stable and coach house with access to the New Yatt Road. Here was housed a 1919 vintage Humber car that Mary drove. It was a two- to three-seater with a dickey and had a very early type of starter. Mary's brother, Selby, owned an HE (Herbert Engineering) of a rather later date. This was a beautiful, hand-made, open four-seater very few of which were produced. Bert used an AJS motorcycle combination. In these early twenties, I was able to use the Adler with my uncle's permission and I sometimes borrowed my Uncle Percy's Hillman 10; it had an appalling clutch that frequently broke half-shafts.

DP 3523

A 14 hp four-cylinder HE (Herbert Engineering), one of only a very few made, owned by Selby Taylor.

Mary in the Singer at Cassington.

About 1923 I bought my first car, a small Calthorpe of about 1913 vintage which had a light two-seater with wood disk wheels; I owned it jointly with Jimmy Hill who subscribed half the cost but used it very little. He used the Rover, owned by his sister Maud Joslin, in which I had taught him to drive. The Calthorpe had a lot of defects but gave us a lot of fun. It was in this car that Jimmy, Denis and I set out for London early one morning. Before we had gone many miles a front spring broke. We cut a branch from the hedge at the side of the road, roped it onto the car and drove on to London, then back again, without further incident. Another time, I took the car out after some adjustments and found that the throttle had jammed wide open when I was nearing the end of a cul-de-sac bounded by a stone wall! The car was eventually bought by Håkan from Sweden, who was engaged to my cousin Phyllis.

The next car that I owned was a 1920 Singer with a back axle gearbox which apart from a noisy timing gear and frequently tearing apart fabric universal joints, was in very good trim and served me for some time. I bought it for about £80 from Myson in Cromwell Road who told me that it had completed the Land's End to John O'Groat's run with the aid of a dynamotor starter on steep hills. I sold it to a parson at Aston.

I travelled many miles with Walter Hewitt who had first a Parry two-cylinder and later a 1913 de Dion; both were very harsh to drive but we travelled happily to tennis matches and once to play hockey at Clanfield. I had very little money but I managed to get a great deal of enjoyment from life probably due to a great extent to the generosity of other people, all of which I seemed to take for granted. I remember a most enjoyable holiday in Devon when I stayed with Maud Joslin's parents, the Hills, at Town Farm, Bratton Fleming. We started from Caswell, Jimmy driving the Rover with Maud and my cousin Jessie Bartlett, whilst I rode a Triumph motorcycle which I believe Jimmy wanted delivered to Devon. We agreed to change over halfway and I rode the motorcycle as far as Taunton, during which time it rained and rained. After Taunton, when it was my turn to drive the car, the sun came out for the rest of the day! During our stay, we went almost everywhere, including Lundy Island, it was an excellent holiday and it cost me nothing!

Another red-letter event was a visit to Wembley exhibition. This, as well as many other outings, were all due to the generosity and hospitality of Maud Joslin. There were frequent journeys to London either by road or rail; we went to exhibitions such as the Motor Show, the Ideal Home Exhibition and badminton finals at the Horticultural Hall. I wonder now how we had time for it all. I maintained my interest in shooting going with my Uncle Percy or Knill Symonds to Caswell, Corsehill and other places where they had rough shooting and trying for duck at Farm Mill. The old quarry in Dark Lane was still quite wild and overrun with rabbits; here I broke the stock of a gun I had borrowed from Denis. Uncle Percy bought me a good twelve-bore gun from Hitchman for £4.10.0 and I bought one from Buckingham at Park Farm for £6; when I became engaged to Mary, I sold this to buy an engagement ring!

Little was accomplished without much physical effort

In the background of all these diversions and amusements, was the necessity of earning a living, which was far from plain sailing. The relationship between my Uncle Joe and de Vinny did not improve and the conduct of the business was not conducive to successful results. I was impatient to acquire more responsibility and anxious to look after contracts on my own. De Vinny was not unhelpful but obviously I could not expect any great enthusiasm from him and my uncle was cautious of my inexperience. However I did gradually gain some supervisory experience and my uncle gave me far more responsibility than I realised at the time. Under his guidance I was closely connected with work on farm buildings, water supplies and improvements at Ardley for A.A. White and I was allowed to use my own initiative regarding rock blasting and well boring there. Other jobs that come to mind in which I was involved with my uncle, were Minster Mill and Vicarage, Moreton, Blockley, Oddington and Shilton. Although I visited many other sites with de Vinny, I was not involved so closely with these.

I did manage to achieve the control of a few small jobs which I was anxious to look after entirely on my own. I have no illusions about the results of some of these early efforts. The work was completed more by luck than any skill on my part, but I learned many lessons and was fortunate in being able to profit in experience at others' expense. A number of early efforts come to mind including the building of a fireplace and chimney at Caswell; this was part of the conversion of an outbuilding into a sitting room. In spite of many alterations and experiments with the flue, the fire always smoked. The formation of a garage in an existing stone building at Ramsden House suffered from a weakness of a bressummer that I designed, whilst the formation of a squash court in an existing barn for Capt. Raikes at Burford was attended by some difficulties in marrying stone slate and asbestos roofing with new glazing in lead-covered bars on the roof. At Burford, there was a house at the top of the hill to which new stone bay windows had been added; here I gained much worry and experience from the persistence of the penetration of driving rain through new stonework.

These were the days when little was accomplished without much hard physical effort, there were few mechanical aids available to help with the day-to-day routine of building. Cement was contained in 2 cwt jute sacks which had to be lifted. Barrows were made of elm, had narrow iron wheels and even when empty, were heavy; on anything other than a hard surface they needed wheeling planks. All scaffold was laboriously erected with heavy wooden poles for which holes were dug or which were placed in tubs filled with soil. The poles were tied with rope or wire lashings and rent-wood putlogs carried the planks. Scaffold poles were often bought 'un-barked' which meant that the bark had to be removed with a draw knife. The best and straightest poles were put aside and used to make ladders in the yard, where the elm barrows were also made.

Concrete was mixed by hand on bankers, turned over, dry then wet, with shovels. Excavation, moving soil and loading were all accomplished with shovels and pecks. Lime, lime putty, road dirt and hair were all basic materials. Gravel as dug cost about 4/- per yard delivered and walling stone about 6/-; out of this quoins were chopped for about 1/- per foot rise. Stone slates, taken from old roofs, cost about £4 per thousand and sawn ridge was about 1/6 per foot run. Wire-cut bricks from local brickfields such as Chawley, Wheatley or Aston Magna were delivered by steam wagon whilst three-inch pressed Peterborough bricks came by rail; all had to be unloaded by hand and thrown, two at a time, along a chain of men. Sand was screened or washed by hand. The use of hand-trucks was common. Bricks and mortar were carried on the shoulder, in hods, up ladders and along scaffold. Barrows were wheeled up sloping runways and heavier weights were hoisted by means of a fall-wheel and rope. We had our first concrete mixer, a Parker Little Giant, about 1924.

I have mentioned that the supply of stone slates was from old roofs; I do not remember ever using new slates. The quarries at Stonesfield, which were no longer worked, had at one time been the main source of supply for the area. Stone of a suitable type was found here in deep quarries and it was brought to the surface and left to weather; in frosty weather it was kept wet until it laminated. I have been told that the stone was never allowed to dry out but was kept covered with turf until it was subjected to frost. Slates from Gloucestershire were sometimes found on local roofs; they were thinner, smoother and of a more sandy colour than the Stonesfield ones. All stone slates were bought and sold by 'long-count'; that is all those over sixteen-inch ('elevens') counted as five units. Normally about 500 were recovered from a square of roofing but it would take about 700 to re-slate it. Running out was done by a labourer with experience who used a notched stick to measure the slate from the peg-hole. The edges were dressed and any broken slate re-holed.

Slate Sizes & Names

The notches on the stick represented the courses and were interpreted as follows: sixteens 24 inches long, short sixteens 23 inches, fifteens 22 inches, short fifteens 21 inches, fourteens 20 inches, short fourteens 19 inches, long twelve 18 inches, short twelve 17 inches, long eleven 16 inches, short eleven 15 inches, long whippet 14 inches, short whippet 13½ inches, long nine 13 inches, short nine 12½ inches, long bachelor 12 inches, short bachelor 11½ inches, long beck 11 inches, middle beck 10½ inches, short beck 10 inches, muffity 9½ inches, long cutting 9 inches, short cutting 8½ inches, long cock 8 inches, middle cock 7½ inches and all up 6½ inches.

The slates were hung on wooden pegs, made by tying a cube of oak or pine with string and then splitting it into square pegs. These were a tight fit when hammered into the holes in the slates, which were then hung on to rent laths spaced to suit the varying courses. When the roof was slated, the underside was torched with hair mortar. After about 1925 the wooden pegs were superseded by copper or cast galvanised pegs, the rent lath gave way to sawn battens of varying thickness and brattice felt was used underneath.

Valleys were 'swept' which meant slating with slates wider at the bottom than the top and bonded with the courses. Hips were either close cut on lead or covered with stone crest sawn to a flatter pitch than the stone ridge. No tilt was used at the eaves; the first eaves course was nailed to the plate which was set in from the face of the wall and the first course on the rafters rested on this. Verges were pointed and not under-cloaked at that time and the stone ridge was bedded on mortar. It was thought necessary to remove moss from roofs when this grew extensively and the operation ('mossing') was carried out from ladders hung from the ridge and resting on bags of softening; the moss was scraped off with trowels and the roofs then brushed with birch brooms.

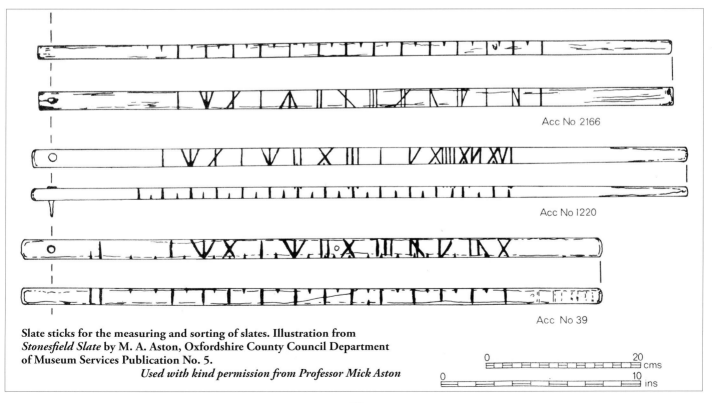

Acc No 2166

Acc No 1220

Acc No 39

Slate sticks for the measuring and sorting of slates. Illustration from *Stonesfield Slate* **by M. A. Aston, Oxfordshire County Council Department of Museum Services Publication No. 5.**
Used with kind permission from Professor Mick Aston

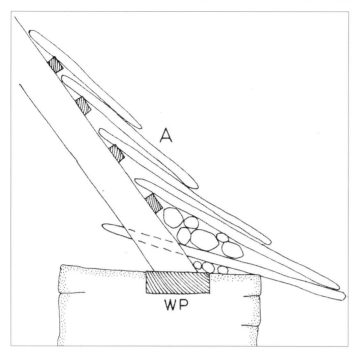

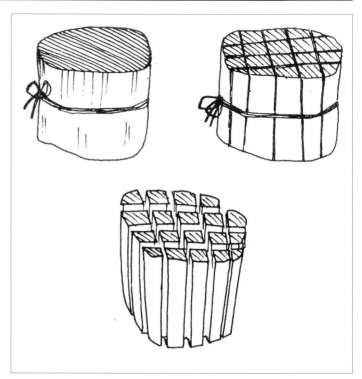

The use of slates at the eaves. Although this diagram differs slightly from the description in Barry's text, it provides a clear picture of an arrangement of slates at the eaves.
From Stonesfield Slate, *with permission from Professor Mick Aston*

Producing the pegs for slating.
From Stonesfield Slate *with permission from Professor Mick Aston*

Water supplied from the mains is now taken for granted on most sites but in the early 1920s there were very few water mains outside urban areas. Before any building was commenced, some thought had to be given to how water could be obtained. The most usual source was from a well which had to be dug. On gravel sites with a high water table this was comparatively simple. The well was quickly sunk and walled up with dry stone or brick; the water was kept down in the final stages by a hand pump. Planking and strutting were seldom used and falls were frequent, however when pre-cast concrete rings became available, these were lowered into position and allowed to drop by excavating under them.

Deep wells were very much a major operation; they were costly and not always successful. Digging through rock was expensive but depths of over 50 feet were commonplace. The positioning was often haphazard and decided by a whim of the landowner or architect who thought water could be obtained where it was convenient to have a well. I recall one at Wootton, near Woodstock, that was sunk to over 80 feet through rock before being abandoned and filled in.

The use of dowsers or water diviners was quite common but they were often unable to estimate accurately the depth at which a supply of water would be found; I am convinced that this ability to detect water is possessed by many who are unaware that they have this skill and that it can be developed, but I do not think that it can be acquired. Personally, in spite of many attempts, I have never felt any indication, but if I hold a rod and a dowser places his hands quite lightly on my wrists, the behaviour of the rod is unmistakable. My cousin Denis Bartlett had the ability to a marked degree and I have spent many hours with him tracing watercourses. My Uncle Joe also appeared to have this ability to detect the presence of water although I never saw him use any orthodox method; he always carried a walking stick and he appeared quite capable of indicating where a well should be sunk. The summer of 1921 was a very dry

one and I well remember him deciding, with complete success, on the positions of several wells which were then dug through rock and clay.

At Ardley there was a costly failure; a well about 30 feet deep that had been in use for a number of years proved inadequate for the farm and went dry during the hot summer. A diviner from Oxford was employed who indicated a strong spring lower down; he estimated this at not more than 15 feet below the existing bottom. We never found water although we dug through rock and clay layers to a considerably greater depth, even driving headers because he insisted we had passed the stream.

All these wells were dug by hand, the spoil being brought to the surface by bucket and fall rope; this was also used for jumping drills through rock. What could not be removed by wedges and sledge-hammer, was blasted. A hole, drilled at a suitable angle and depth, was used for a fused charge of gelignite plugged with clay and, as sometimes several were fired simultaneously, this required careful timing. The shots of about 4 or 6 oz were wrapped in waxed paper and the detonator, crimped to the fuse, was pushed in; normal fuse rate was about one foot per minute, with instantaneous fuse connecting the charges. Usually I did the preparation myself. It was important to make sure that all the charges had exploded. One of the difficulties was keeping the charges dry under water, as the pumps had to be stopped and lifted up before firing. Eventually I solved the problem by enclosing the shots in old cycle tubes. Later on I devised a means of firing the detonators by wiring them to a coil and battery; this was crude but effective. At appreciable depths, it was necessary to allow time to clear pump stagings and ladders which would otherwise have suffered from flying rock; the greatest risk was going down to retrieve a charge containing a detonator that had failed to explode.

I had no experience of deep well boring with diamond drills, but both my uncle and grandfather had used this method to considerable depths and the equipment was still in the yard. The drill heads were studded with industrial diamonds and were carried on 1¼ inch or 1½ inch screwed tube. The driving equipment at the head of the well was in a heavy wood frame and the drills were lifted by hand under some form of shear-legs. I have regretted that I did not get more information about this from my uncle, but I assume that power must have been obtained from a portable steam engine which was also used to operate a pulsometer pump. The well between 71 and 75 High Street was bored with this equipment, as was the Apley Barn bore for Witney town supply; this bore hole was sited between the Burford Road and the river Windrush near the junction with Tower Hill. Where there was a suitable spring that would provide sufficient head of water, the installation of a 'ram' to lift the water to suitable storage tanks provided a reliable supply. Storage tanks were also fed by wind-driven pumps installed over the wells.

I spent most of my time out on site

Witney, at this time, was a pleasant town to live in. It was not overcrowded, the population being about 3,500 and there was a comfortable and relaxed association between most people. A walk through the streets was enjoyable, there was no congestion or rush and cars or cycles could be conveniently parked. The conduct of business was courteous and usually on a personal basis and although everyone worked hard, there was much satisfaction in what was accomplished. The present day rush and tear of life did not exist, those one did business with were relaxed and most people seemed happy and contented.

Between employers and those they employed there seemed to be a spirit of loyalty and cooperation which resulted in good will, each seeming to understand the others' problems. Everyone worked hard when work was available. Competition was fierce and profits small with little margin for waste of either materials or time; if there was no work or the weather prevented work being done, men had to be stood off with resulting loss of wages. There were no paid holidays or overtime rates but we tried to provide regular employment, particularly in winter time, and skilled men were often glad to do other work in order to be kept employed. When things were slack, we tried to provide work and sometimes this was unprofitable but I like to think that our efforts were understood and appreciated. Everyone had to stand on their own feet independent of subsidies and no one expected something for nothing; some unemployment at times was accepted by many and was not generally a reflection on a person's ability.

At the first sign of a job being started, a number of men usually presented themselves at the site in the hope of being offered work. A few men could also be found near the centre of the town who were eager to start any work offered. Labourers presented themselves equipped with peck and shovel whilst tradesmen, of course, had their own kits of tools. All were prepared to travel a reasonable distance to work, if necessary on foot or cycle, in their own time; walking or riding time was only paid to those who were employed regularly and moved from site to site. This was calculated on the basis of one hour's pay for each mile travelled beyond a three-mile radius from the yard; thus a man working at Leafield would be paid about eightpence a day.

Wages were usually paid on Friday or Saturday for the time worked up to the end of the previous day. Tradesmen claimed an extra half hour to sharpen their tools. The calculations were simple and done in the evening so that money could be drawn from the bank and paid the next day. Termination of employment was by one hour's notice which could take effect at any time but was usually given one hour before knocking off time on Friday, when a 'back day' was included in the wage paid. In spite of the apparent harshness of these conditions, our relationship with employees was good; I do not think we exploited the surplus of labour and look back with pleasure on the friendly spirit that prevailed.

The average workman lived in conditions that would now be considered unthinkable; water was drawn from wells, waste deposited in a hole in the ground, food cooked on an open range and oil lamps and candles were usual, although a few homes in the Urban District had electric light. The workmen appeared to be content with life, were honest, and they helped one another. Self-denial and discipline were commonplace and they achieved satisfaction in what they did. Now we are surrounded by devices and machines that are supposed to make life easier and more comfortable. The state defends us against poverty and disease but in spite of all this, many people still fail to achieve any kind of contentment or happiness.

In the early twenties, the conduct of business was comparatively simple, trading was straightforward, the employer undertook to do work for a certain payment and he received this payment in cash or by cheque without deduction. Later on he was expected to pay some income tax, if he had made a profit after paying his overheads. These consisted of rent, rates, insurances and the maintenance of plant, tools and property; property was also liable to schedule A tax. All this could be assessed accurately. The workforce received their wages at an agreed weekly or hourly rate with a small deduction for a contribution for a stamp on an insurance card. Goods that were purchased were listed and priced at rates that could be expected to remain static for a long time and the seller who could produce them a little more cheaply had a competitive advantage.

The welfare of the town and public services provided were controlled by the Urban District or Rural District Councils although the County had certain responsibilities for main roads. These bodies were run efficiently and at very little cost to ratepayers. Rates were low, for example the whole of the yard, including the house lived in by my uncle, cost about £40 for the year and the house we occupied in 1929 cost about £13 for a year. The affairs of the Urban District were looked after by the part-time Town Clerk and a surveyor, George Eaton, who had a small office in the Corn Exchange; he had a boy to help him. The whole of rural affairs were under the care of Basford who had a small office at the Blanket Hall. He had the help of an assistant, Baston. The affairs of the County were under the control of a man named Mould who lived in the New Yatt Road; it was the late twenties before they had a small yard and office in Gloucester Place where the entrance to Ash Close was made later.

The mid 1920s were times of great activity in which I was concerned in some way or another. Quite a lot of work was undertaken by the firm though most of it was looked after by de Vinny. I was also busily engaged in trying my wings in obtaining, supervising and organising some of the work on my own initiative. Around this time the firm was engaged in jobs at Bampton (a house and farm), Charlbury and Eynsham (schools), houses at Headington (Lucas £1,200, Weston £2,000, Tucker £1,000) with Crease (£1,000) at Sandford Road and others in Divinity Road and London Road. Extensions were undertaken at the Wingfield

Brashfield House, Bicester, 1927.

Hospital and work done at Oddington, Waterloo Farm, Steeple Aston, Churchill, Cumnor, Ardley, Coxwell, Minster, Begbrooke, Leafield and elsewhere. Under my care was an extension at Brashfield House, Bicester, for the Maitlands under a London architect. This was a nice stone-built extension with freestone dressings and oak joinery carried out in two stages in 1925/26. At the same time, I designed and built a small farmhouse near Heyford; this I am pleased to see has now been pulled down. I was not pleased with the results of my efforts.

Towards the end of 1926 I met Sidney Smith and his architect, Oliver Hill and preliminary negotiations were started in connection with the building of Merryfield House in the New Yatt Road for which a tender was submitted. Prior to this, the firm had built a number of houses adjacent to Early's mill in the Burford Road for the Witney Mills Housing Society; this work was negotiated by de Vinny who carried out the contract quite successfully I think, but the harsh red roofs were regarded as an eyesore. I think there were twenty houses which cost about £500 each.

Around this time, I was also actively engaged in buying and selling secondhand motor cars. These I acquired in London mainly through my cousin Jack Bartlett although I had some dealings with a man called Pickthorne. I became familiar with the dealers' activities in Warren Street and Euston Road, where there was a great deal of kerbside dealing and I am surprised that I escaped with un-burnt fingers! Most of the cars I kept only for a short time but a few served me very well for longer periods.

This dealing in motor cars produced a certain amount of profit and I added to my capital by undertaking some small installations of shafting and electric motors and by constructing a few wireless sets.

In August 1925, Mary and I had become engaged and the acquisition of money became of prime importance for the future. My position in my uncle's business was still a very minor one, but towards the end of 1926 de Vinny was becoming more and more dissatisfied with the outlook and obviously he sensed that the business would not support the two of us. To be fair to him,

Car Dealing

Amongst the cars that went through my hands were: a Calthorpe 1913, a Singer 10, a Calthorpe Coupé, a Hampton with a Meadows engine, a Lagonda with a snub nose, a Standard 9, a Rover 9, a Morgan, an Alvis four-seater, an Alvis 12, a 1921 Morris, a Morris Chummy, a Singer Sports, a 1925 Morris, a two-seater AC, a Morris Oxford, a Standard 14, a Clyno 10, an MG sports, a 1927 Morris, a 1926 Morris, a Fiat four-seater, another Standard 9, a Fiat 10, a Standard 11.9, a Bean, a Talbot 14, a Riley 9, a Singer Sports, a Swift Sports, an Austin Seven, a Riley saloon, an Austin 12, a Swallow Standard and a Riley 12 with Wilson gears. Later for my own use I bought a new Flying Standard, three Triumph Dolomites, a Talbot Ten, a Ford 8, a Vauxhall 14, a Morris 14, a Wolseley 14, a Singer 1500, a Ford Zephyr and a Zodiac which I used until after 1945.

he was never unpleasant in his relations with me and he acted in a perfectly straightforward way in all his dealings with my uncle, although they disagreed over many things.

In January 1927 a start was made on the building of Merryfield House in the New Yatt Road for Sidney Smith, although the contract was not actually signed until February. This was by far the largest contract in which I had been directly concerned. The quantities were prepared by Dearle of London and Bartlett Brothers submitted the lowest tender; I made several visits to their offices before a final figure of about £6,000 was agreed. I had sole control of this work from start to finish. Although I made mistakes, I can look back on a reasonably successful result due, to a large extent, to the loyal cooperation and skill of the men employed.

Oliver Hill was not an easy architect to work with. In many ways he lacked practical knowledge and appeared to me to be more concerned with the external appearance of the elevations than with the practical construction or the convenience of the internal arrangements. It is not for me to criticise the outcome of his design, which was generally very much admired, although there were critics

Merryfield House 1926/27. *Above, clockwise*: **Building the chimney; the rear elevation with Sidney Smith and Dorothy Bartlett in the doorway; Merryfield House, Sidney and Dorrie to the right of the front door with the building team including the foreman, Reg Franklin, (slightly right of centre).** *Below*: **Glazing in progress.**

of the comfort and convenience after it was lived in. Dorrie (my cousin Dorothy Bartlett) and Sidney were married in September 1927 and moved into the completed house. I cannot remember any particular difficulties or anxiety in achieving completion by this date in spite of being involved in a great many other matters during this same period.

After due notice de Vinny left on May 21st 1927 to start a small business on his own. Later on, he built himself a house in Puck Lane where he had a small yard that he had purchased from Earlys. Until his house was completed, he continued to live in the house belonging to my uncle at 31 Gloucester Place. I think he made himself a living but he never achieved anything spectacular; he confined his activities to jobbing work and a few single houses. He closed down after the outbreak of war in 1939 and later on, during the war, we employed him as a site agent when we built the hospital at Bradwell Grove. Finally, he retired to live in the Isle of Wight where he lived on into his eighties. I always had a soft spot for him and although we became competitors, we always got on well. After he left, I had much more responsibility.

I became more than busy but still found time for other activities. On January 8th 1927 my Uncle Oswald reached the age of 50 and I went to a party of 50 guests which he held somewhere in Chiswick. I joined the golf club at Buckland where Selby and Bert Tanner frequently played. I spent a lot of time on the river at Rushey, played much tennis and badminton, went to dances and made frequent visits to Wigston where my Uncle Will lived at St. Wolstans. I also visited my mother who was staying at Elmside in

Wimbledon. Since my father's death in 1917 the house had been let furnished for short periods, which augmented our income, but it was becoming increasingly difficult to arrange a satisfactory tenancy; between lets there was quite a lot of work which necessitated my mother staying there. After my grandmother died in September 1927, it was decided that the contents of Elmside should be moved to Witney and in June 1928 my mother gave up her home and the house was let unfurnished.

Business was becoming more demanding. We were building a number of houses at Leafield for Chipping Norton Rural District Council; the surveyor, A.T. Green, later came to the Witney Urban District Council in the same capacity. These houses were looked after by my uncle, but there were many other sizeable projects that I handled. Around this time, I remember buying stone slates for about £3 per thousand, quarrying stone at Marriott's Farm to obtains lengths of over four feet, taking many risks including handling and placing very heavy pre-cast rings at Brize Norton with quite inadequate tackle and being underneath shear legs when they collapsed over Wootton well; I tried to be in a vast number of places at the same time.

Soon after de Vinny left, I got a telephone (Witney 84) installed in the office. The staff then consisted of Cousins and a boy from Bampton named Townsend. In the autumn, I managed to have a few days' holiday in Devon. Returning through Chippenham, I was diverted by floods caused by a vast amount of rain accompanied by gales. Amongst many other troubles, the weather brought to light a weakness in Merryfield House. The gales and rain were driving water through the external walling with resulting damp patches. The specification called for the local stone walling to be built with a rich mortar of cement and sand; no one realised that this, although producing almost the strength of a fortress, channelled any moisture through the walling. To make matters worse the stone was freshly quarried and porous and the joints were not pointed but raked off leaving a surface which invited the entry of water. Local practice was to build stone walling with soft lime mortar which 'breathed' and with the joints pointed with a trowel finish. The green stone eventually weathered and sealed itself, resulting in complete freedom from damp but architects without local experience thought they knew better. Some time later, I refused to build some walling at Leafield Radio Station under a Ministry of Works architect who asked for some unusual construction; it is easy to be wise after some defective construction has come to light, but I have found that it is often the builder who is remembered for the defect and seldom the designer.

When the houses at Leafield had been completed, more were started at Stanton St. John. There was work for Oxfordshire County Council under Bill Daft who was then County Architect and for the GPO at Witney and Charlbury. We submitted a tender for a new bank at Witney for Lloyds under Wallers of Gloucester. In the early twenties, they had started a branch managed by Savage in a house near the Buttercross. Later in 1927 Harold Mace took it over and came to live in one of the houses that we had built in Gloucester Place.

On Christmas Day 1927 (a Sunday) a heavy snow storm began, resulting in deep drifts blocking most roads. Selby and Bert, who had been staying at the Chestnuts, had to return by train, leaving their car behind. Jack Bartlett, after trying to get through, had to return from this side of the Chilterns. I think Uncle Oswald finally managed to get through with his car on the following Wednesday,

but for a few days nearly all the roads were impassable. It was nearly a week before we managed to reach Charlbury. I tried with Jack's Vauxhall and got as far as Minster but I recall driving through a single track with snow 4 or 5 feet high on each side.

The following year was less eventful but very busy. Cousins was running the office side very well and I spent most of my time outside on sites. Cousins still lodged in the end cottage in Mill Street with the Dix family. In 1926 he had married their daughter and his daughter Valerie was born in 1927; they all continued to live in the same cottage. We both used a short cut to it through Long's Yard off Gloucester Place, over the wall and across the garden; this only took a few minutes from the office.

Commencing with the building of Merryfield, contracts were numbered for any work that we considered of major importance and by the end of 1928 about 35 had been undertaken including: Lloyds Bank, Police Station extensions, Marriott's wool store, Bampton police houses, Asthall Farm, Burford Hospital, Standlake Rectory and School, Leafield Radio Station extensions and maintenance, schools, farm repairs, roofing and Post Office work. There were also houses at Wootton, Leafield, Stanton, Heyford, Burford Road, Church Green, Standlake and Crawley Road amongst others. The work amounted to about £28,000. All this kept me busy but we made very little money. There were many difficulties and not the least was always the acute shortage of cash, but I was happy and had many other interests.

Bampton police houses.

I still dealt in motor cars and I remember providing a new Riley Saloon for someone named Youens at Coombe. This was the first brand-new car that I had ever handled and I drove it from London with great pride. I delivered it to Coombe the next day where I collected their old Morris Chummy in part exchange. The Morris was sold to my Uncle Percy and served him well for some years.

There were frequent journeys to London and Wigston. The trains were frequent and reliable: from Witney there were seven trains in and out each day, at 7.40 a.m., 10 a.m., midday, 3 p.m., 5 p.m., 7 p.m. with the last about 10 p.m.; goods traffic was equally fast and reliable.

We found time for holidays and spent happy times away when we could get a few days off. Mary and I stayed at Hunstanton with the Godwins in June where there was bathing, fishing and other attractions of the seaside. We played golf and visited the surrounding countryside including Sandringham. The Godwins were friends who had lived at Witney, Harold Godwin had been a cashier at Barclays and later they moved from Hunstanton to

Brize Norton School, Barry on the right.

Sutton Bridge where we often visited after we were married. In the autumn, before any of us married, Mary and I stayed at a farm at Lower Aylescot accompanied by Jimmy Hill and my cousin, Jess. This farm was then isolated and hard to find; the next habitation, about two miles away, was called 'Little Comfort' but both couples had cars and we enjoyed visiting the surrounding areas of Devon. Our hosts, the Chuggs, became great friends and did their utmost to feed and entertain us royally; we had good company, a good garage, a pony to ride and rough shooting on the farm, all for 30/- a week. The stone house was typical of many in Devon. It was built in the protection of a valley with farm buildings grouped around it. It had a large projecting entrance porch and was both comfortable and warm but also cool in summer. It was heated by log fires, lit by lamps and candles and had water pumped from the stream which lower down, had the indoor sanitation built over it! This type of holiday was the forerunner of many well-remembered breaks that Mary and I enjoyed in later years. We were seldom away for longer than a few days, at the most a week, but we visited many places and crowded in a great deal of enjoyment.

During these early breaks I began to rely more and more on Cousins to look after business affairs while I was away; I soon found that he was able to accept a great deal of responsibility with ability and common sense. With the advent of 1929, contracts were in being for work that maintained a sizeable turnover but still produced only a very small profit. The contract numbering had risen to 68 and included several large jobs in Witney, a new house at Appleton for Basil Blackwell (£4,789), one at Woodstock for John Brooks (£1,000), a lot of work for OCC, HM of Works (HMOW), breweries, farms and schools.

A cat in the larder

In April 1929, de Vinny left the house at 31 Gloucester Place and moved to the one he had built in Puck Lane. I had agreed with Uncle Joe that I could have the house at a rent of £40 per annum on a quarterly tenancy, as Mary and I were making preparations to get married in June. Very little was done to the house beyond some decoration and alterations to wiring, but a great deal of thought was given to the acquisition of furniture within the limits of the money that we had available and a visit to High Wycombe produced results at wholesale prices. A bedroom suite in good quality oak, two easy chairs, a settee, a set of walnut dining chairs, three carpets and a walnut sideboard cost little more than £100. We had an extending dining table from Wimbledon, Mary brought several pieces from the Chestnuts and we were fortunate in having many small essentials given to us such as china, glass, cutlery and silver. Several items were bought at sales, for example a kitchen table for 7/6, chairs for 12/-, a mahogany swing mirror for £4 and a wall mirror for £1. All in all it did not create any financial embarrassment; every article was simple and inexpensive and we ended up with all we needed.

We were married on June 1st 1929 at Cogges Church by the Rev. Hudgell; the Hudgells were friends of the Tanners. Mary said that she would like to be married at Cogges so in order to conform with the residential qualification, they invited her to sleep at the Priory one night, for three consecutive weeks. This she did, complaining afterwards that the room she slept in was haunted and that she was

Mary Taylor.

Barry Taylor.

disturbed on each occasion! I am open-minded and have no fixed opinions because I have never experienced any indication whatever of the presence of anything supernatural. Although I laughed about it at the time, Mary herself was quite convinced that she had heard and experienced something unpleasant. I must admit that the room where she had slept was in the older part of the building, right away from that occupied by the Hudgells. In any case, the whole of the Priory is steeped in history and an ideal setting for anything of this nature. I was not aware until many years later that the incumbent who followed Hudgell, the Rev. Spence, owned a dog that in no way could be persuaded to enter this particular room.

After we were married, we set out for Berrynarbor, in North Devon and stopped the night at Glastonbury. The next day whilst travelling across Sedgemoor we had trouble with the car, a 10 hp Fiat, which necessitated removing the radiator. At an isolated farm I was given every assistance and was able to strip down the front of the engine in a barn while Mary was entertained to tea in the farmhouse. These were the days when any trouble on the road produced unstinted help from complete strangers and there was a spirit of camaraderie and mutual trust which was seldom abused. I can think of many instances when I was helped, towed, provided with materials, facilities and petrol (and a can) with complete trust and no thought of reward.

Our stay at Berrynarbor was not without incident. On the first night we were disturbed by a commotion accompanied by breaking of crockery and other noises which were, we were told at breakfast, 'due to a cat in the larder'. However it was soon evident that the disturbance was attributable to something more serious and was in fact caused by the husband of the proprietress attacking her with a knife! He suffered from some form of mental instability, was put

Mary in the doorway at 31 Gloucester Place, Witney.

The garden, 31 Gloucester Place, with Witney Mill's chimney rear left.

under sedation by the doctor and taken to Barnstaple where later we took his wife to visit him. Apart from this incident we enjoyed our stay there and had ten days of delightful weather. On our return home we were welcomed by my mother and went to start our married life at Gloucester Place.

Looking back one is inclined to retain only the happy memories which are part of the whole picture of the comings and goings of many visitors. I recall the early morning and the sound of horses being called from grazing in Marriott's field, the chestnut tree in full bloom, the shade of the sycamore trees over the lawn and sunsets over the cornfields to the west. It might be said that these houses that we had built in the Close, together with the terrace of houses known as Cape Terrace, which extended Gloucester Place from what was a yard off the High Street, were part of the beginning of the expansion of Witney from its original plan. However, there was then little sign of the rash of development that was to come later. To the south and west of 31 Gloucester Place the outlook

was unobstructed as far as the buildings in Corn Street, with the workhouse and the water tower the only outstanding features in the open country. I have heard it said that the wind blew straight from the Bristol Channel!

We were happy, we were busy and we looked forward to the future but in July we were saddened by tragedy. I had sold the Fiat car to Jimmy's brother, Tony Hill, and until I purchased another car, I was using a borrowed Sunbeam motorcycle. On this I was returning one morning from Rollright up Finstock Hill when a child ran from an opening on my left which led from the school. Although I instinctively swerved to the right, I struck the child. His home was almost opposite the lane, but I think he died before I carried him there. His name was Ezra Pimm. He was about four years old and the nephew of Aubrey Pimm who worked for us as a slater. Although at the inquest I was exonerated from any blame, I shall always feel that had I not swerved he might have escaped serious injury. I did not ride again.

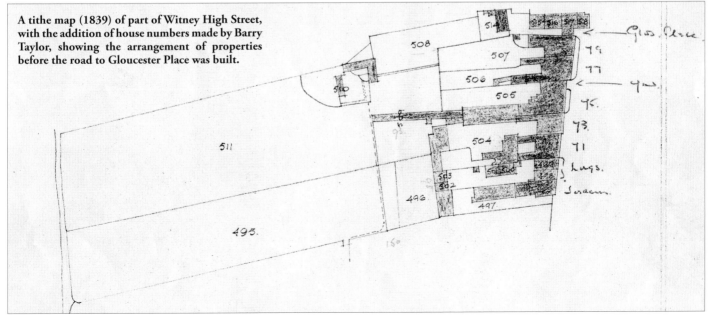

A tithe map (1839) of part of Witney High Street, with the addition of house numbers made by Barry Taylor, showing the arrangement of properties before the road to Gloucester Place was built.

My future was dependent on the success of the business

I cannot say that business was flourishing but we still maintained about the same turnover. Around this time I remember well some of the larger jobs such as the telephone exchange at Abingdon, the new short-wave transmitting station at Leafield Radio Station, a house built for the Misses Hollyer on Cumnor Hill, with glorious views, extensions to 'Falaise' nearby and later, a large house for Sir John Fisher Williams built in Pullens Lane. There was work at Wigston, looked after by my uncle, the rebuilding of Cogges rifle range and a small sausage factory for Uncle Percy. The exchange at Abingdon, the work at Leafield and some other Post Office contracts were carried out under the old HMOW. I recall some

Abingdon telephone exchange c.1930/31.

Falaise, Cumnor.

72

Leafield Radio Station, short wave building 1930 and (*right*) two views inside the station.

of the Clerks of Works that they employed. The one at Abingdon, Adair, was honest and generally helpful but he let nothing slip and made sure that he received a sound job, for which he was respected. Webber, who looked after Leafield, was bombastic, difficult to pin down to decisions and often intimated that he could make things easier if he received something for himself. Another, Farleigh, had the reputation of being difficult to satisfy, but I think his bark was worse than his bite and although he required a first class job, I found him perfectly fair, reasonable and honest.

Although we were doing a lot of work, there was still very little profit; 1928 and 1929 had produced some, but in 1930 it was almost nil. It was around this time that, after many discussions

Pullens Lane, Headington

The image of the Buttercross has been made with Percy Bartlett's own, personal stamp.

Right: One of the pie wrappers.

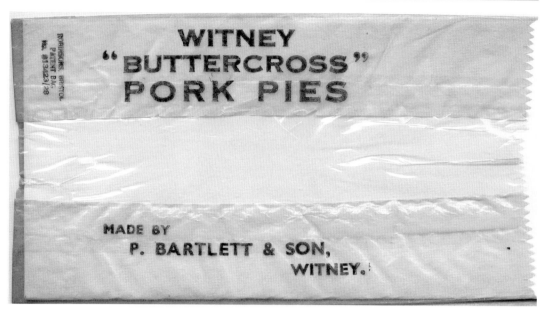

WITNEY "BUTTERCROSS" PORK PIES

MADE BY
P. BARTLETT & SON,
WITNEY.

Percy Bartlett's shop in the Market Square, Witney where he sold his own brand of Buttercross sausages and pies. Later his recipes were bought by George Brazil who, with the help of Percy's son Dick Bartlett, expanded the business at Brazil's factory in Corn Street, Witney.

between my uncle and his brother Uncle Ern, it was proposed that I should be given a financial interest in the firm and that a company should be formed with my uncle taking a less active part in it. There was much journeying to and from Wigston where my Uncle Ern was living and Uncle Will agreed that he would provide some more capital by a mortgage on the land at the old aerodrome (the freehold of 75 High Street was already mortgaged). The accountant, Austin Moody, gave my uncle some very sound advice and he was also very helpful to me but I was not altogether happy and finally put forward a scheme that would give me control; in this I had Moody's entire cooperation. I was able to provide a small amount of capital and eventually my uncle was persuaded to agree to give me control.

I provided £500 in cash and entered into an agreement to purchase the goodwill, fixtures, plant and office furniture for £1,000, together with the book debts and the stock at valuation, all paid for over a period with interest. Thus I was able to take over the business as a going concern and pay out of the profits. I was granted a lease of the yard and office for 14 years commencing at a rent of £100 per annum. This arrangement was intended to operate as from the financial year ending March 1931, but when the accounts for this period were received they showed that up to this date things had become much worse. The gross profit had dropped to under £400 which entailed a loss of about £1,000. Both my uncle and Moody were dubious as to the wisdom of proceeding with the transfer. However I had the confidence of youth and I was quite prepared to stand or fall by my own efforts; probably I did not realise how much

Mr. J. Francis Bartlett,
75 High Street,
Witney,
Oxon.

Dear Mr. Bartlett,

As promised in my letter of yesterday I enclose herewith Statement of the Accounts of your Business for the year to March 31st 1931 and I am very sorry indeed that they show a most disastrous result for there is a Loss of nearly £900 which I cannot understand.

Extract from Austin Moody's letter dated 9th May 1931.

A further extract from the 9th May letter.

Extract from a the letter dated 27th July 1931 – about the transfer of the business.

was at stake, but I can remember no anxiety or doubt, in any case things had gone so far that it was difficult to imagine any alternative and I was only too keen to throw off the fetters.

After further discussion it was eventually agreed that I should start trading on my own as from June 30th 1931, however the agreement was not actually signed until August 25th. It was part of the terms of the agreement that in addition to the £500, a further sum should be paid on August 24th to make up the total of the trade creditors owed at June 24th. As my uncle had already received £482 of this, I paid an additional £458 to make up a total of £1,440. This left a sum of £2,660 for me to pay to complete the total purchase money which had been agreed at something over £4,000. I gave a promissory note for this amount to be paid in half-yearly amounts with interest on the outstanding principal at 5%.

I was now in control of a business that had most of the essentials of a going concern but which was losing money fast. From this nucleus it might well be asked how I expected to make a profit and be able to pay off outstanding debt. My uncle was left with the properties, the Yard and the house, 75 High Street, six houses in Gloucester Place and the buildings and land at the aerodrome, all of which were producing rent and all of which were mortgaged. In spite of his doubts and misgivings as to his wisdom at relinquishing control of the business, he was at last able to relax to a certain extent. He had a moderate income for those days and as far as his health would allow,

he enjoyed another 15 years of fairly active life. At this date, June 1931, the total value of his freeholds was shown at £9,500 on which a total mortgage of £6,500 existed; the net total of his assets was shown to be £5,214. This excluded 71 and 73 High Street, because these had not been conveyed to him. When my grandfather Joseph Bartlett died in 1910 he left no will and a deed of family arrangement was drawn up appointing trustees to administer the estate for the benefit of my grandmother during her lifetime. This postponed the right to freeholds to which my uncle, as the eldest son, would have been entitled on his father's death and enabled my grandmother to receive income. At her death, she was able to leave furniture and personal effects to be divided between her children.

When my grandfather's brother, Christopher, died in 1918 he left a will giving the whole of his estate, subject to a few minor bequests, for the use of his nephew (my uncle), Joseph Francis, for his lifetime. However, if he died childless, the estate was to be sold and divided between his nieces and nephews. This created a trust which made it very difficult for my uncle to continue to trade and to finance the business by a mortgage which existed on the freehold of the property. In 1921 another family arrangement was made between all the nephews and nieces in which they agreed to give up all their respective rights and interests to my uncle for a nominal sum. Subsequently the freehold and personal estate of Christopher were freed from the trusts of the will. This seemed a fair and reasonable solution to avoid a break-up of the estate. It gave my uncle title to the freeholds and other assets and deprived the rest of the family of any future claims on the estate. In effect, it was what Christopher had intended and providing that the estate did not depreciate in value and providing my uncle bequeathed it to his brothers and sister no one would have suffered any hardship. In fact when my uncle died in 1946 all of them were living and his estate, left equally between them, amounted to about £30,000.

I had no doubt whatever that I could make a success of the business; when we are young we can sometimes be very confident of ourselves. I had given much thought to the innovations that I intended to make and I had discussed these in detail with Cousins but a great deal of the incentive was provided by the prospect of unfettered control. In the past I had been fully aware that my future was dependent on the success of the business. My relationship with my uncle was good but there is little doubt that his influence had a

ESTABLISHED
1852

TELEGRAMS : BARTLETT BROS., WITNEY.
TELEPHONE : WITNEY 84.

Contractors to H.M. Office of Works.

BARTLETT BROS.

(E. BARTLETT TAYLOR)

Builders, Contractors,

Decorators,

Hot Water & Sanitary Engineers.

75, HIGH STREET,
WITNEY,
OXON.

OUR REF.

YOUR REF.

Bartlett Bros. letter heading c.1931.

restraining effect and it may also be that I was not really providing all the effort that I was capable of. Few people lack the power to improve their position but sometimes what they lack is the will to do so; where this will exists what they accomplish is largely a matter of great effort combined with positive thinking. First must come sufficient incentive to create the will. I was brought up to appreciate the value of money because there was never much of it, however it was never of prime importance and acquiring it often took second place to many of the diversions which make life enjoyable. The prospect of having sufficient money to accomplish those things that I wanted to do provided a natural incentive but it never entered my head that I should ever acquire a surplus beyond my immediate needs.

One of the delusions of this world is that having money makes one happy; to those in want the prospect of having money in the pocket can provide a feeling of happiness and the lack of money can be the cause of suffering. By itself it can never take the place of those things that make life satisfying and provide tranquillity and contentment. If we aim to give help where it is needed and to leave behind engravings of kindness and consideration on the hearts of those with whom we associate, then the use of money can sometimes alleviate the burdens of others. It is not wise, however, to be deluded by the apparent simplicity of this way of providing help.

Up to the time when I assumed control of the business, I had a great many other interests. We had a wide circle of friends and Selby and Bert often stayed at the Chestnuts with their families. We played golf at Buckland and spent much time at Rushey Lock and on the river. There were tennis parties in the summer and badminton in the winter with much travelling to matches. Oxford was a convenient playground with dances, the theatre and indoor skating. Journeys to London, Wimbledon, Wigston and Oadby were frequent. I remember returning on one occasion with a large picture tied to the side of the car; my Aunt Lydia had died in 1928 and amongst her bequests to me was a large oil painting by Hall of Newmarket which she had prized. All of her silver was left in trust for me after the death of her nieces Mary Bloodworth and Lily Howitt. They generously suggested that we should have it during their lifetime, so we were able to use this, together with items that Mary brought from the Chestnuts, soon after we were married.

We were far from being well off and I have always appreciated how fortunate we were in being able to enjoy some of the finer things in life and, under Mary's skilled management, to maintain a standard of living far beyond that which might have been expected from our very limited income and position.

I had now been with the firm ten years. The intervening years had been very full, I had learned a great deal and I had been very happy, now I had the opportunity to use my initiative freely. I knew I must grasp this chance with both hands. We are given opportunities, we have free choice and free will in our thoughts and actions. We can take the tide at the flood and plunge boldly in or put off any decisive action by irresolution and let the chance slip by without realising what we have missed. I was aware that my future was in my own hands, that all my thoughts and energies must be concentrated on the business. I was fortunate in having the full cooperation of others, in particular Cousins, who was also prepared to work long hours and devote the whole of his energy to the same ends.

Lily Howitt (left) and Mary Bloodworth.

At the Witney aero club tennis courts.

Part Four
PEAKS & TROUGHS, 1931-mid 1970s

I managed to find a body that more or less fitted

The control of the business was virtually in my hands from the end of June but I have already mentioned that the agreement and other documents relating to the transfer were not signed until August 25th 1931. I well remember this day because I had visited some sites around Oxford and had kept an appointment with an eye specialist named Adams at the Cardinal's Hat. To examine my eyes he dilated the irises which resulted in me being unable to see clearly for some hours. I was unable to read clearly, but I was well aware of the contents of the document that I signed. I had given considerable thought to a programme of events that would follow and I had discussed everything very fully with Cousins.

We had already put in hand work that would provide better office conditions. The old office adjoining the gateway was retained as a reception area and staffed by a boy (Beale). Cousins and I were installed in a new office that had been formed at the east end of the joiners' shop which was on the first

Top office 1933.

floor. This gave an area of about 20 square feet, divided from the shop by a fireproof wall, with access leading from a covered stairway. I have clear memories of the long hours we both spent there in the evenings and weekends, when we found that we could achieve a vast amount of work without interruption; with an early morning start and most days taken up with general organisation, there was normally little time or opportunity left for concentrated thought.

One of our first tasks was to reduce overhead costs and we embarked on a programme of very drastic pruning of all expenditure that was not productive. A review of the stock in the yard showed quite a number of items that were unnecessary and we decided to hold an auction sale. This took place one Saturday in October. A great many people came because they were curious, but we sold all the lots and received a total of about £150, which was more use to us than dead stock. Following on from the jobs that I had agreed to complete, we obtained a fair share of work; competition was fierce but we went out and got work by personal contact and by the end of the year we could see a small overall profit.

One of the contracts that we negotiated was an extension to the weaving shop at Early's mill where it was necessary to excavate thousands of cubic yards to extend the existing floor level. To cope with this, we used a drag-line excavator with a 50 foot jib. Whilst

To Mr. J. F. Bartlett,
75 High Street,
Witney, Oxon.

I promise to pay to you or your Order for value received the sum of Two Thousand, Six Hundred and Sixty Pounds (£2,660) by twenty equal instalments (£133 each) on the 24th day of June and the 24th day of December in each year, the first of such instalments to be payable on the 24th day of June 1932 and to further pay with each instalment Interest at the rate of Five Pounds (£5) per centum per annum upon the Principal sum for the time being unpaid. One year's Interest to be paid with the first instalment. Should default be made in the payment of any instalment for a period of twelve months of its becoming due the balance then outstanding shall immediately become due and payable together with Interest as aforesaid.

31 Gloucester Place,
Witney, Oxon.

December 11th 1931.

Promissory note dated December 11th 1931, from Barry to his Uncle Joseph.

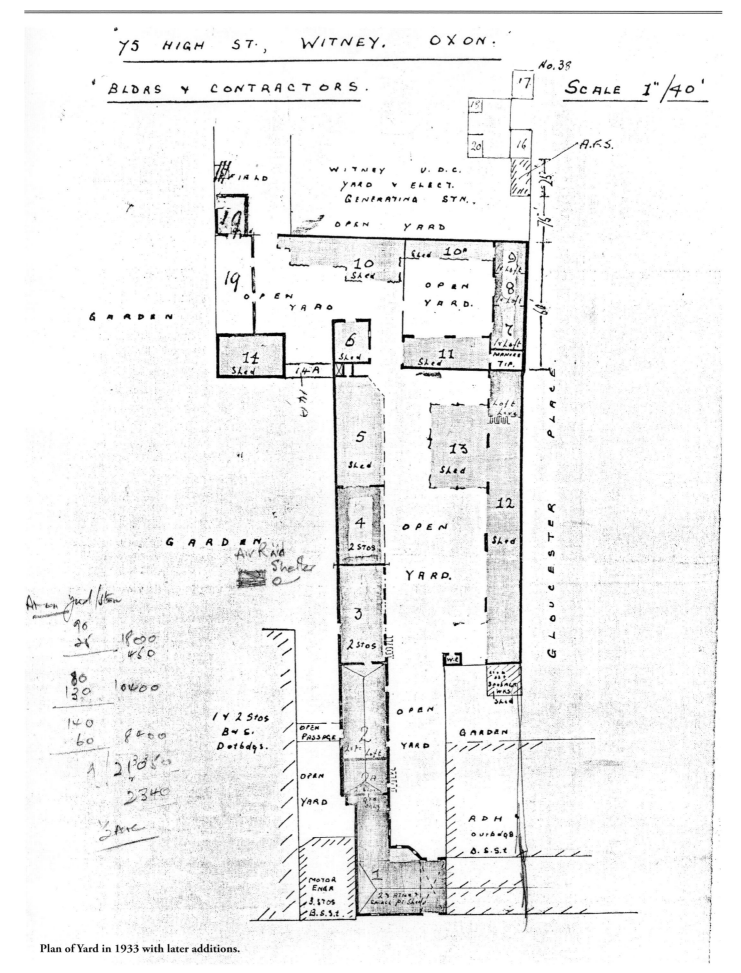

Plan of Yard in 1933 with later additions.

Extension work at Witney Mills.

getting this on to the site, we overturned it! When we had it back on its tracks, it coped very well and we used a fleet of Albion chain drive lorries, hired from Haines, to remove the spoil. Another dragline experiment was tried out at South Leigh; we worked at the Church, the old vicarage, the new vicarage and what was known as the college where there was a small lake which we undertook to clear. I asked the blacksmith to make up a small bucket that could be pulled by a horse and this worked quite successfully. We built a garage at Witney for the Oxford Bus Company which was our first experience of industrial building and this led to another similar garage at Thame for the same company. By the end of our first tax period, April 1932, the accounts prepared by Moody showed an encouraging result with a turnover of £7,261, a gross £1,279, overheads of £683, leaving us a net profit of £596.

I still played some golf and a lot of badminton. I still bought and sold motor cars but I had given up playing much tennis in the summer. In the spring of 1932, I smashed up the Swift car near the MG works on my way to Abingdon. The insurance company decided it was beyond repair but I retained the salvage and later stripped the chassis and

straightened it in the blacksmith's forge. After reassembling it, I used it for a time before selling it for about £50. I was also driving a Singer sports car which I enjoyed. This reminds me of another Singer that I bought after it had been in a fire; the body and everything else that was consumable had been destroyed but I managed to find a body that more or less fitted, reconditioned the engine and got it going again. I don't know how I found time to do all this because I was very busy in many other ways.

We had decided early in 1932 to make a joiners' shop in the old saw pit shed. We installed a new timber front with windows facing the yard; these gave a north light resulting in a well lit building with north and south lights already built in the roof. The saw pit was partly filled in and used to accommodate a 14 hp electric motor that drove under-floor shafting from which drives were taken to a large 30 inch saw, a combination machine (moved from the old shop), a planer, a morticer as well as a spindle driven by a separate motor. The planer and spindle were reconditioned machines purchased from Cooksleys and the big saw I bought from the Electricity Company at Aylesbury. I remember driving over to purchase this and finding a lorry on the Thame road, managed to persuade the driver to turn round, collect the saw and deliver it to Witney for £1. I think the total outlay on all the machines was less than £150. We sold the old spindle for £5 to a man called Powell in the Cowley Road in Oxford.

Witney bus garage.

Thame bus garage.

Above & right: **Bicester School 1933.**

I fitted all the machines and shafting myself and after concreting the floor and fitting wood covers over the ducts, we had a useful shop with machines and eight benches on which we made our own joinery for many years. The first foreman who we trained was Ron (Roland) Reed who came to us as a very green carpenter; he was with us a number of years through the war. I believe Harry Turner, who followed him, also had charge of this shop before we moved to the old generating station in 1946. An enormous amount of joinery was turned out during the war and the shop was working long hours and at weekends in order to cope with our requirements.

Left & below: **The joiners' shop, converted from the old sawpit shed 1933.**

Above: Another view of the joiners' shop.

Left & below: Stock house at Smith's Crawley Mill.

I got on very well with Sidney Smith and in the early days of 1932 we did a lot of work for Smith's Mills at Crawley. A new stock house of about 50 feet span was built and floored with blue bricks which included a complicated system of floor drainage to separate the grease (carried over the river); this cost less than £2,500. We also built several new bleaching sheds. These were always a problem in construction because of the action of the sulphur fumes. The old standard construction was in timber, all pegged and without any metal. On the advice of the building research station at Watford, we experimented using brick construction and the use of Delta metal. In spite of their advice, we had much trouble mainly due to the expansion of the mortar which they had advised should be rich (two to one) cement and washed sand. This work at Crawley was followed by large jobs at Bridge Street Mill.

I also got on well with Harold Early and after the weaving-shed extension, we did more work for Earlys at Witney Mills, New Mill and Newland. I found it very difficult to get very far with Marriotts and it was some years before doing any work for them; one of our early efforts was to spray-paint the whole of the exterior of Mount Mills for about £150! Work of a minor nature was done for Walkers at their new mill in the Crofts.

My Uncle Joe was still involved with the old aerodrome; he had sold some of the buildings and land whilst other areas were let. We built a detached house for him on the frontage adjoining the Curbridge turn with the idea of developing the frontage but this was not proceeded with and the house was eventually sold to Jack Wharton. The old transport sheds had been let to someone named Faloon who started a garage and installed petrol pumps. The venture was not successful and when he vacated the site, my uncle let the property to Jack Wharton at a rent of £2 a week.

At the end of our first full year, April 1933, the accounts showed the turnover had risen to nearly £12,000. Overheads were about £1,100 which resulted in a net profit of £1,640. We were doing a large assortment of work, some of it as far away as Thame and Bicester, but a great deal locally; we were beginning to gain a reputation for efficiency and good workmanship. We had invested in spray-painting equipment which we used extensively on large areas in factories and schools; it brought some troubles with it, but on the whole it brought us work and covered large areas very quickly. When Miss Gray first opened it, the whole of the interior of the Bay Tree Hotel in Burford was distempered for £50 and the whole of Marriott's Mount Mills was externally painted in two weeks.

When the Radclyffes first bought Lew House, we did extensive work for them under their own architect. We undertook extensive alterations at The Marlborough Hotel for Collett, additions for

Aero House.

May 17th 1933.

Mr. E. Bartlett Taylor,
75 High Street,
Witney,
Oxon.

Dear Mr. Taylor,

Herewith I enclose Statement of Accounts of your Business for the year to March 31st 1933 and really must congratulate you upon such an excellent result of your year's work.

When the figures were completed I was extremely surprised for, although I anticipated you would improve the Business, I scarcely expected you would effect such an extraordinary improvement within so short a time.

Extract of letter from Austin Moody dated 17th May 1933.

The Yard 1933.

The Yard 1933.

Mrs Corley on Woodgreen, new houses for Dring, Cook, Barrell, Pickford, and Shuffrey with houses also at Aston and Burford Road. We did considerable work on property owned by Brooke, Cruley and Mrs Walker and much farm work for colleges and other owners at Cote, Aston, Leafield, Bampton, Langford, Hailey and South Leigh. There was work at the glove factory at Witney and Charlbury as well as other industrial work at Aston Laundry and all of the blanket mills. We held the maintenance contract with HMOW for the area which included Leafield Radio Station.

Chevrolet with Charles Monk and Bert Basson.

Right: The Timber Store 1933

Below: The Timber Store 1935

This was a time of consolidation. I cannot recall any large contracts (over say two or three thousand pounds) but we managed to achieve a turnover of about £15,000 in the year ending 1934. This was largely managed from medium and small jobs near home. I did most of the supervision on sites myself as Cousins had no transport; this was very time consuming but we had no other travelling supervisor. A great many jobs had only a charge hand, so it was advisable to try to cover all the sites at least every day or so. I would cover an area in the morning and another group of jobs in the afternoon and probably all or nearly all the sites on Friday or Saturday to pay wages.

To illustrate the number of journeys I undertook, a typical day in 1934/35 would start with a visit to the glove factory in Newland, Witney to check the alterations. Next would be a visit to Stanton Harcourt Road to see the work on a pair of houses for Miss Mawle and a bungalow for Cyril Mawle, followed by a call at Cogges Priory to view work done for Rev. Spence. After this a visit to check a well being sunk for J. Dee Bury near Ballast Hole and then across the track to High Cogges, where Bernard Bury lived, to view work on the farm and cottages. The next call was at Wayside Cottages on the road to South Leigh where thatching and repairs were underway. Then on to South Leigh School, the Church, Rev. Freeman's house and Channing Pearse's school; this included a walk through the churchyard and garden which provided me with a little time to relax. From there to the village where a few small jobs were being undertaken for Miss Bliss, Miss Penson at Bryans and to Warner's Cottages, by the level crossing, where work was in progress for Brasenose College. I then drove on to College Farm to Trevethan's and to Blue Barn for the College. Sometimes I might go on to Sutton Farm and Beaumont's house and then cut across to Aston where we were sinking another well, then back via Ducklington – another well, that was bored to over 70 feet producing only contaminated water. To complete the morning I would visit jobs being done in Witney for example Swan's house in the Crofts, The Marlborough Hotel, Well's new shop front, the Home Maid shop and the Angel and Star public houses. An afternoon would take me in another direction with fewer sites further afield.

We came into contact with quite a few architects some of whom we worked with repeatedly over many years; a number became personal friends and I could tell many stories about them. On the whole they were efficient and exacting but they knew what they wanted and what was in the best interest of their employers. They were fair, understood our problems and what is so important most of them knew how good work should be done. Many of them had no transport and had to be taken from the nearest station to the various sites. My early memories are of Tommy Rayson, Gilbert Gardener, Bill Daft, Harry Smith, Russell Cox, Sam Cripps, Thorpe, Openshaw, Wilkins and later partners Arnett and Knight. Of those from London I recall Maule at Hook Norton Manor, Ford at Brashfield House, Bicester, and Collins at the Home Maid shop. The latter used to come to lunch at 31 Gloucester Place and was known to absent-mindedly try to pocket his table napkin. I almost forgot Oliver Hill who I found difficult to work with but who became so famous.

As well as architects there were many others, such as quantity surveyors, bursars and surveyors with whom we had much personal and friendly contact. In particular I would mention Green, Basford and Geary, the Urban District, Rural District and County surveyors who for so many years did a vast amount of work almost single-handedly. In those days the responsibilities of the local authorities were many and when I look back on the small numbers of staff that accomplished so efficiently what they had to do, I am astounded by the numbers who now fill the buildings of these local authorities.

In 1935 we built the two storey timber store that stands in the middle of the open yard, and about this time we purchased a building site opposite the Water Tower on the Burford Road. This was a triangle of land that we hoped would eventually provide a site for a public house that Clinchs were considering building. In the office another telephone was installed, we employed a cleaner and provided an electric fire!

I had hazy ideas about buying a helicopter

When my uncle sold the hangar at the aerodrome to Charles Early, I think he must have let him have some additional land. In the 1930s a company known as Berkshire Aviation started flying from what had been the war-time airfield; I believe at this time they used the hangar that had been sold to Batt. Later, about 1932/33, this was taken over by a company calling themselves Universal Aircraft Services and with the acquisition of yet more land, which must have been bought from the Gallaway Trustees, they started flying aircraft for training purposes. The king pin in this company was D. L. Townsend who had a manager there called Saunders.

The land was owned by a company known as Witney Estates which was controlled by Laurence Wingfield, a London solicitor. I believe Charles Batt was associated with both companies; Witney Estates also owned Downs Farm, which was let to Jim Sheppard. It is likely that all the land was acquired at the same time.

In June 1934 a club was formed and operated as Witney Aero Club Ltd with Townsend as Chairman. We built a clubhouse for them in 1934. Membership of the club cost £2.2.0 a year and flying about £1.10.0 an hour with dual instruction for under £2. In those days I was interested in anything to do with aeroplanes and had flown in the old war-time type of Avro. When the club was formed I joined and did some flying in a dual-controlled Cirrus Moth with an instructor named Slade. He was a very good instructor, we got on well and had a lot of fun but I found it difficult to find the time to fly. After I had flown solo in the summer of 1934, I did little

more for some years. Slade was succeeded by Walters with whom I had one or two refresher flights but I did not obtain my licence.

As well as building the clubhouse we, from time to time, did work for Universal Aircraft Services Ltd. In this connection I had common interests with Townsend and Saunders and met a number of club members socially, some of whom had their own aircraft; we had enjoyable times including a garden party with two hundred guests where I met the Duchess of Bedford and a number of others who, at that time, had a claim to fame. I had hazy ideas about buying a helicopter and using it to visit our building sites and got as far as trying out a Piper Cub. In the end I realised that the whole idea was impractical. As well as training commercial pilots and maintaining aircraft, Universal Aircraft Services let off part of the hangar and workshop space to someone called Willoughby who was building an experimental twin boom aircraft later known as the Willoughby-Delta; this was a prototype of a delta wing aircraft of which I will write more later.

By March 1936 our turnover had reached almost £19,000 and although we had no outstandingly large contracts, there was a steady flow of work with quite a few sizeable jobs. We were still doing a lot of mill work, particularly for Smiths. We became expert in the construction of large grease settling tanks; these were about 15 feet square and built up of 3 inch timber bolted from top to bottom. We made up a machine in the shop for jig-drilling the wood which was then assembled at the site onto brick bases and jointed with white lead and mill bond.

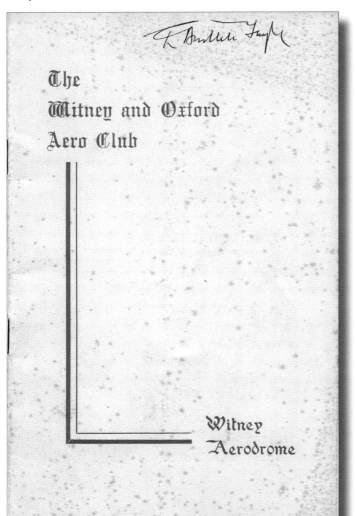

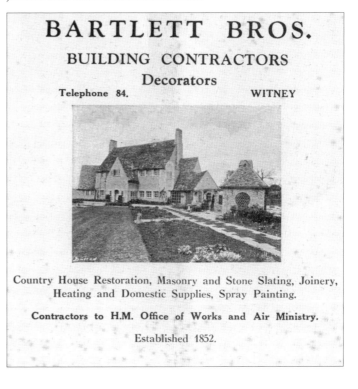

Left: The Witney and Oxford Aero Club booklet cover (reduced).

Above: An advertisement for Bartlett Bros on the back cover showing the completed Merryfield House.

The clubhouse for the Aero Club built 1934.

We also carried out a lot of work for the Oxford colleges, often a series of jobs in one area for example: at Stanton St. John (Queen's College), South Leigh (Brasenose College), Black Bourton (Lincoln College), Northmoor (St John's College), Sutton (Merton College) and Challow Marsh (Lincoln College). Other work that covered a long period was at the Marlborough Hotel for Percy Collett where we were working almost continuously for over two years. Around this period up to early 1936, our activities also included major alterations and additions at the Lamb at Burford for Stockley under Russell Cox, a new telephone exchange at Woodstock, a new house at Northmoor for Ireland and a new house in Dark Lane for Hedges (this was a two bedroom house, complete in every way, for £300). We undertook alterations and improvements at Caswell to provide a new kitchen and bathroom and also did work at South Leigh at St. James's and at Tarwood House (including a squash court). We were also involved with additions and improvements at Hook Norton Manor for Crossmans the brewers under Major Maule, a new garage and forecourt (known as Tower Hill Garage) on the Burford Road in Witney for the Thomas brothers; this was built on the site of a gravel quarry that was sold to them by my Uncle Percy and Knill Symonds. Under Oliver Hill, there was reconstruction work and additions made to allow for more bedrooms at Merryfield House with a new detached stone built house nearby for Edith Smith.

Other construction work was as follows – alterations and additions at Wadley Manor and Lodge under Thorpe for Hon. Mrs Craven, improvements at Lew Farm and cottages for the Radclyffes, alterations and additions at Hopewell House, Burford and for Lady Gwyre at Swinbrook, new cowsheds and improvements at Challow Marsh under Thorpe for Lincoln College, a new house for the headmaster at Chipping Norton School, modern intensive piggeries at High Cogges for Bernard Bury (here we laid cold asphalt floors which were a complete failure and had to be replaced with asbestos cement slabs), a pair of bungalows at Curbridge for

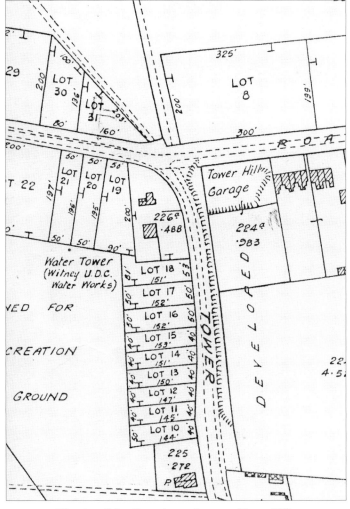

The site of the disused gravel quarry, Tower Hill.

The house for Chipping Norton School.

Allsworth, rebuilding a barn at Standlake for Pickfords, a sewage system at 'Red City', Long Hanborough for North (here we had considerable trouble with split concrete rings leaking), work at Smith's, Walker's and Early's mills and at Leafield Radio Station, a number of projects on public houses for Hunt Edmunds brewery and work on the oldest building in the area, Yelford Manor, which was then used to house farm workers and infested with fleas. Later in the year we started building council houses at Bampton for Witney Rural District Council and a new house for Western at the Deanery, Bampton, a studio at Thames House, Eynsham, two houses for Joe Beaumont at Sutton, another extension to the Home Maid and much other work including a new building for Universal Aircraft Services which they called Witney Aeronautical College to which I will refer again later.

In the spring of 1936 I bought my first new car, a Flying Standard, which I collected from the Standard works at Canley. I cannot remember what it cost, probably about £250. Later this same summer, Cousins bought a car from the Thomases, an 8 hp Morris in which I taught him to drive, at least I went with him on a few short journeys and then left him on his own!

It was about this time in the spring that I was ill with tonsillitis and was at home for about a week and Dr Timings came to see me. Shortly after I thought I had recovered but after a few weeks I was bad again and I remember being so shaky that I was unable to open

Witney Aeronautical College.

the garage door. After this we arranged to go away and we were able to share a bungalow with the Godwins at Looe in Cornwall. It took me a few days to recover but I soon picked up and we were able to have an enjoyable holiday; by June I was in full swing again.

During the winter months I was still playing a lot of badminton; in addition to playing at the club and for the club in matches, I played in tournaments for the county team (Berks, Bucks and Oxon). All this entailed a lot of travelling. In men's matches my partner was usually Jack Lawton Smith and in mixed matches, Dot Smith (Walker). We travelled many miles in Dot's Rover 14, an excellent car, which she later changed for a Triumph Continental. At this time I was using a Triumph Dolomite of which I had three in succession.

Geoffrey Armitage, who lived at Sutton Courtenay, owned the building known as the Old Gaol at Abingdon; he had made some very good badminton courts in it and formed a club with a select membership. To here, with boundless energy, we travelled at least once a week to play. Badminton was very much part of my life until the outbreak of war in 1939. Although Mary did not play to the same extent, she often travelled with us and I have very happy recollections of trips to Dudley, Amersham, Cheltenham, Banbury and Bristol where we were entertained with meals and parties and made many, many friends.

At the side of the hard tennis courts and amongst the buildings (which belonged to my Uncle Joe) on the west side of Witney Aerodrome was a squash court that had been left unfinished; Universal Aircraft Services rented this from my uncle and we plastered and completed one court for them for the use of Aero Club members. It was lit by a petrol-driven lighting unit. Here I played squash with a number of enthusiasts including Charles Batt, the Leytons (who were doctors), Armitage from Abingdon and Brian Walker. I was also able to use the court at South Leigh College, which was a wooden one. Here I frequently played at weekends with Jack and Neville Smith and another fellow also named Smith who lived at the College; I remember playing a match against the College team and being entertained afterwards to tea.

We were becoming prosperous and undertaking larger contracts which required more mechanical plant. At first I used other contractors such as Diezel for excavating and moving spoil; at Hailey Road School we paid 1/6 per cubic yard for this and it was the first contract on which we used large dumpers. We were buying materials in larger quantities – cement in 100 ton lots, paint in 100 gallon lots and timber, under an arrangement with Ingrams, direct from the docks at Gloucester.

I had an idea of starting a builders' merchants' business and explored the possibility of renting the adjoining shop (73 High

Hailey Road School, Witney under construction 1937.

Above: **Frilford automatic telephone exchange (100 lines).**

Right: **Burford automatic telephone exchange (the first 200 line type).**

Street) from my uncle. I am ashamed to say I sounded out Badham, who was W.H. Ingram's representative, to see if he would leave them and run a business for us. Fortunately he refused because I do not think I had enough capital or knowledge to make a success of it. I think Bill Ingram knew I had asked him but it never came between us and they continued to be one of our largest suppliers; they helped us in many ways for years.

For some years we had many associations with the General Post Office (GPO). We rebuilt Witney Post Office and Sorting Office and did work at Charlbury Post Office, Abingdon Post Office and also built a new telephone exchange there. We maintained Leafield Radio Station and built a new short-wave station. Later on, we built a number of the first automatic telephone exchanges in rural areas including Woodstock, Bampton, Eynsham, Frilford, Burford, Middleton Cheney, Shipton, Leafield, Carterton and Standlake. Later still we built the larger stone-built type, for example at Minster Lovell.

It was in the early days of 1937 that I acquired a Triumph Dolomite car; it was a demonstration model with a very low mileage and it was by far the best car that I had so far owned. At that time I was doing a high mileage, the car was fast, comfortable and served me very well. However towards the end of December, while travelling from South Leigh to Sutton on a slight covering of snow, I met a large milk lorry on the corner of Blue Barn Lane. Although I got out of his way by throwing the car into the lane, he slid into the side and crushed me against the bank. The car was a complete write off. I immediately ordered another similar car and collected it from the works the following week. I ran this new Triumph for over 120,000 miles and had another similar one during the war, this I bought secondhand, as a spare, but never used it and sold it unlicensed in 1946. I also had a nice little Talbot Ten which I bought during the war and stored it in the garage at the Chestnuts after filling the engine with oil.

Barry's Triumph Dolomite, No. 1, registration RD9058.

In a less happy condition after a collision with a milk lorry between South Leigh and Sutton early in 1937.

Three more views of the 1937 accident to the first Triumph Dolomite.

Right: The second Dolomite seen with Barry and Mary at Amberley, Gloucestershire.

The third Dolomite after registration, ELO 7.

Hendon Air Pageant 1937.

We found ourselves in possession of a flying school

For some years after building the clubhouse in 1934, we undertook all the development required by Universal Aircraft Services at Witney Aerodrome. In June 1937 we completed a new building that had been designed to accommodate students who were taking courses in aviation. We agreed to a schedule of payments on specific dates which also carried interest. These lagged behind and by November we were pressing them for payment. After several meetings that John Welch attended, it became obvious that they were unable to meet the payments. In January 1938 a creditors' meeting was called. After some discussion, it was divulged that they had received an offer for all assets they owned at Witney Aerodrome and the liquidator proposed that this offer should be accepted as no other had been received. I objected to this because in the first place I did not consider that it represented anything like the true value of the assets and furthermore the offer was made by people who were obviously connected with Wingfield who had an interest in both Witney Estates and Universal Aircraft Services. Probably the intention, having got rid of the liabilities of Universal

Aircraft Services Ltd, was to continue to run the aerodrome by the company registered as Witney Aeronautical College Ltd, which was controlled by the same directors.

Over many years I had been mildly interested in anything to do with flying and this had been increased by my association with club members and with others connected with the flying world. One of the highlights of the year was a visit to the Air Pageant at Hendon and we got to know many people who had the same interest. I was on good terms with Campbell Russell who was the chief instructor at Witney and he introduced me to Beatrice Macdonald, the wife of Allen Macdonald, who lived at Hythe Croft, Eynsham. Mrs Macdonald owned her own aircraft, a Miles Hawk, which she kept at Witney; she held a B licence and was a competent instructor. I think it was Russell who sowed the seeds and after a great deal of discussion, in which John Welch took a prominent part, we decided to make an offer for the assets of Universal Aircraft Services. This offer was accepted by the liquidator and we found ourselves in possession of all the stock in trade of a flying school, with a lease of the landing ground and of all the aerodrome buildings at Witney. I remember walking round the hangar one Saturday morning early in February 1938, everything was deserted and very quiet. I looked at everything we had bought and went home to lunch thinking to myself 'whatever have I done now'!

With the assistance of John Welch, Jane Macdonald and Russell we organised some of the old staff who had agreed to remain with us. We were able to continue to give training facilities to the pupils enrolled on the various courses and to provide them with accommodation at the college; this residential mess was run by a Mrs Spencer who looked after the catering and agreed to continue to manage it for us, which she did very efficiently. Of the remainder of the old staff we had 'Mac', by which name he was always known to everyone, who did all the odd jobs, cleaned the aircraft, swept up in the hangar and workshops and made himself invaluable in so many ways. He slept in the hangar, fed in the mess and was caretaker and watchman. He seemed content to spend all his time

At Hendon in 1937. The aircraft to the right, K5540, appears to be a Hawker Hart of 605 County of Warwick Squadron.

Witney Aerodrome 1938, with Hugh Olley striding in on return from a flight.

on the aerodrome. His real name was Macduffel and he appeared to have no relations or ties; I think we paid him the princely sum of £2 or £3 a week and fed him.

The chief engineer, named Lofthouse, decided to leave so we promoted Harry Martin, who lived in Witney. We never regretted giving him this responsible position. We soon engaged a manager named Cowan; he was young and full of enthusiasm but was inexperienced and proved unsatisfactory. We found a flying instructor named Olley who was first class in every way and I will write more about him later. In the office we employed Mary Clark, a daughter of Harry Clark the local ironmonger. We had an engineer called Older, who lived in Abingdon, and the assistant engineer was Huntley, who lived in Witney.

Courses of instruction continued to be available for flying training for pilots' A and B licences, for the instructors' course, navigators' licence, telegraphy and telephony, ground engineers' A & C licences and parachutes. Olley and Jane Macdonald handled all the flying training whilst Russell and Martin covered the ground engineering and allied training; Russell held a pilot's B licence as well as his other qualifications.

When we built the college it was decided that the clubhouse, which had been sited on the east side of the landing field, should be moved. This was done by jacking it up and moving it bodily on rollers onto new foundations adjacent to the college; the buildings were then linked by a covered way; this gave the club members

better facilities for meals etc. and the pupils taking courses, who were also club members, were able to use the club bar.

The Witney & Oxford Aero Club was a separate limited company and when we acquired the lease of the freehold with the assets of Universal Aircraft Services, this gave rise to the position whereby the club members had no clubhouse or facilities for flying and we had no connection with the club. Early in March, John Welch, Piggott and I met the shareholders in West's office in London and agreed to purchase all the shares in the company for their paper value which had been agreed between our accountants, Critchley, Ward and Piggott, and West; we were also offered the recently formed company, Witney Aeronautical College Ltd, for a nominal figure. This we refused because we had already formed a new company known as Witney Aerodrome Ltd in which Jane Macdonald and I each held equal shares; this company was registered on 7th April 1938. We therefore had equal shares in two companies, this and the Aero Club. I was not particularly concerned in the day-to-day running of either but the general organisation took up quite a lot of my time and I was drawn into policy discussions. Cowan was not the right person to continue as manager and I had to tell him; this he took very well and we remained on friendly terms, in fact he came to see me several times up to the outbreak of war. He was replaced by M. Goring Benge who made a good manager; he coped very well with all the problems that beset us and was efficient and popular.

WITNEY & OXFORD AERO CLUB
LTD.

MINSTER LOVELL
OXON

DIRECTORS
B.S. MACDONALD
E.B. TAYLOR

TELEPHONE
OFFICE WITNEY 170
MESS „ 283
HANGAR „ 234

WITNEY AERONAUTICAL COLLEGE

WITNEY AERODROME · OXFORD

FLYING CHARGES.

Instructional Flying	...	...	...	£1 17 6	per hour
Solo Flying...	...	...	...	£1 10 0	,, ,,
†Contract Rate (Solo)—(50 hours)	...	£1 0 0	,, ,,
Blind Flying	...	...	...	£2 0 0	,, ,,

† Applicable only to British born subjects, in respect of whose training the Club is eligible for Air Ministry subsidy. Contract Rate otherwise 25/- per hour.

Special Note.—It will be observed that so far as the Pilot's "A" and "B" Licences and Instructor's Licence are concerned we do not make an inclusive charge for the courses. Each pupil pays for exactly the flying training which he receives and no more. We consider this the only fair method as on an inclusive basis the pupil who is quick to learn obviously is helping to pay for the slow pupil who requires additional instruction. The figures given below are for an average pupil and are therefore approximate. They include every expense to be incurred by the pupil and there are no vexatious extras. The items marked * amounting to £6:8:6 and £51:1:6 for "A" and "B" Licences respectively, do not normally form part of "inclusive" quotations. This must, therefore, be taken into account when comparing our charges with those of other establishments which quote an "inclusive" price for "A" and "B" Licence Courses.

COURSE 1.

PILOT'S "A" LICENCE (Private Licence).

			£ s. d.
*Pilot Member's Subscription to Club	...	...	3 3 0
10 hours instruction @ 37/6 per hour	...	...	18 15 0
3 hours solo flying @ 30/- per hour	...	...	4 10 0
*Medical Examination ...	...	...	10 6
*Photographs for Licence (passport type)	...	...	3 6
*Air Ministry Fees for Licence	...	...	1 6 0
*Essential Flying Kit (obtainable at Aerodrome)	...	1 5 6
(Total cost for average pupil)			£29 13 6

(Minimum age for Licence: Seventeen.)

Top Left: The cover of the prospectus for Witney Aeronautical College.
Above: The price list of the courses offered at the College.
Below: Believed to be Jane (Beatrice) MacDonald.

Witney Aerodrome, c1939 with a perimeter fence of chestnut hurdles. The aircraft lined up belong to the Witney and Oxford Aero Club. Nearest the camera G-AEHL is a British Aircraft Manufacturing Co. Ltd Swallow L25C Mk II serial number 427 supplied new in September 1936 to Major Norman Holden of Selsey in Sussex and transferred to the ownership of Beatrice MacDonald in March 1939. Next is a Swallow 2, G-AFGC, whose registration was issued in April 1938 and was transferred in January 1939 to Ronald Dryden of Standlake and Hugh Olley of Dryslwyn, Carmarthenshire. This aircraft is still extant, in private hands, in Devon. A third Swallow stands beyond but cannot be identified. The Swallow aircraft were developments of a popular German design built under licence at Hanworth in Middlesex. The last aircraft in the line-up is G-AAKO. This was a DeHavilland DH60G Gipsy Moth, serial number 1045, registered new to the Witney and Oxford Aero Club in July 1937. It seems that it was requisitioned in November 1939.

G-AEHL at the refuelling point at Witney.

The Aero Club building was moved to a position next to the College building as can be seen in the top view and in closer detail, *right*.

Below: Inside the hangar. G-ACZC on the left was an Avro 504N, serial number AX854. This may have been ex RAF who used them as basic trainers. It was first registered for civilian use in September 1937 to Richard Holme of London but its usual base was at Doncaster. Beyond is a De Havilland DH87 Hornet Moth G-AFEC, serial number 8157 registered in May 1938 to Captain Ford of Faringdon. The furthest aircraft in the row appears to be G-ADLO, a Phillips & Powis Aircraft Ltd Miles M2P Hawk Major. In the foreground is G-AAKO as detailed on the previous page.

Inside the workshops of the Witney and Oxford Aero Club. G-EBTZ was a De Havilland DH60 Moth, serial number 437, which in March 1938 belonged to the Worcestershire Flying Club of Pershore. It may have come to Witney prior to going to Pershore.

Two more views in the workshop area. In the view above frames are ready for recanvassing and doping whilst below is part of the machine shop.

Another pair of views in the hangar, G-AAKO stands on the left in the top view. The bottom scene has most of the Aero Club's Swallows parked up. G-AEHL has been seen before, G-AFGE, a Swallow, was first registered to Ernest Bartlett Taylor in October 1938. It was requisitioned in 1940 but survived the war and is still extant. Beyond is G-AELH, another Swallow first registered to Beatrice MacDonald in July 1938. On the far side of the hangar appears to be a glider in front of G-ABAG, a DH60 Gipsy Moth which is also still extant and in the Shuttleworth Collection.

WITNEY AERODROME
LTD.
TRAINING SCHOOL
FOR PILOTS, ENGINEERS, WIRELESS OPERATORS & NAVIGATORS

DIRECTORS
B.S. MACDONALD
E.B. TAYLOR

MINSTER LOVELL
OXON

TELEPHONE
OFFICE WITNEY 170
MESS " 263

No. 339,071.

(COPY)

Certificate of Incorporation.

I hereby Certify that WITNEY AERODROME,
LIMITED, is this day Incorporated under The Companies
Act, 1929, and that the Company is **Limited.**

Given under my hand at London this Seventh day
of April, One Thousand Nine Hundred and Thirty-eight.

P. MARTIN,

Registrar of Companies.

The letter heading for Witney Aerodrome Limited.

Left: The certificate of incorporation for Witney Aerodrome Limited issued on the 7th April 1938.

aeroplane from a field adjoining the house where he lived. The work at Signet Hill led to other contracts under his architects, Eric Cole & Partners. Not only was our turnover increasing but we were making very good profits.

Up to the spring of 1939 I was still playing badminton with great enthusiasm and was selected for a few County matches, travelling as far afield as Harpenden and Southsea but this was my last fling and I never played again after the outbreak of war in 1939.

To revert to the affairs of the aerodrome venture, the first nine months brought many problems and little if any profit. After the Munich crisis, there was much talk of rearmament and the need for pilots was stressed. Soon we were involved in the Civil Air Guard (CAG) scheme which provided subsidised flying training up to A licence standard and we had a great many applications from suitable young men. I kept no record of the total number we trained but it must have been substantial because it became necessary to expand our fleet with the addition of five Pobjoy engined Swallow aircraft which proved very suitable aircraft for initial training. We were also flying the Miles' Hawk, two Gipsy Moths and an Avro Cadet which we hired; there were always one or two machines undergoing Certificate of Airworthiness (C of A) testing or not airworthy for some reason.

We contemplated expanding out activities to an additional aerodrome near Thame and eventually decided to lease part of Kidlington Aerodrome. Fortunately this was never implemented because of the outbreak of war. I like to think that we made some contribution to the training of pilots who flew with the RAF in the early days of the war. In the same way I feel that Bartlett Brothers made some contribution to the successes that were achieved by the RAF by close cooperation with de Havillands in getting the damaged fighter aircraft flying again from Witney.

During the summer of 1939, the Willoughby Delta aircraft was completed and we were flattered when Willoughby asked if we would agree to Olley test flying it. He carried out the initial tests on it, took it into the air and reported that it handled well. Later he flew it to Martlesham for further tests and I believe it was given a provisional C of A. It was on July 10th when he took off with Willoughby after some modifications had been carried out to the tail trim by Willoughby's engineers. After some hours, when they did not return, there was some anxiety and later that evening I found Benge telephoning to try to find out what had happened. After some time, he got a report of a crashed aircraft

There was no mains electricity supply to the hangar and adjacent buildings so power was provided by a generator driven by a diesel engine; with the onset of winter we found that the battery was suffering from old age. I found one of similar capacity at Wyck Hill House, where they had recently been connected to the mains supply. I remember going over to see it one day in December when there had been a fall of snow. The battery seemed in good condition, so I bought it but I had great difficulty in getting out of the drive because of the depth of the snow. After the thaw, we sent Channon over to dismantle it and supervise the carting to Witney where it fulfilled our needs. Problems such as this took time to sort out, but I enjoyed it all, getting things organised gave me a lot of satisfaction.

Cousins was taking a lot off my shoulders and we were getting through a lot of work although I can think of nothing spectacular. We were involved in a number of rural housing schemes for local authorities; we had quite large contracts at Bampton, Eynsham and Northleigh, for example, that added considerably to our turnover. By March 1938 this had reached £29,000 and although it dropped a little the next year, by March 1940 it had risen to nearly £43,000.

During 1938/39, we worked for a long period at Signet Hill for Silvertop who was a member of the Aero Club and flew his own

The Willoughby Delta F aircraft at Witney Aerodrome. Registered G-AFPX in January 1939 to the Willoughby Delta Company Ltd of 56 Moorgate, London.

near Middleton Stoney. I took him and a friend in my car to try to find it. We did indeed find it, spread over a large area near Calcott; both of the occupants had been killed instantly and it was a tragic end to the hopes of those pioneers of the Delta Wing when they were so near to success.

I can remember no official investigation other than the inquest. We collected the pieces and brought them back to Witney but nothing was discovered that could throw any light on the cause of the accident; I think it was generally accepted that it had been brought about by some defect in the trim control. I understood that the Martlesham tests revealed that the centre of gravity varied with speed and this is probably what they were trying to correct by the modification of the trim. However it has always seemed to me that a pilot of Olley's experience would have been quite able to

cope with any instability, unless of course some mechanical defect had locked the control. I remember during the war, flying over Witney with Marshall in a de Havilland Rapide when he suggested that I should move my weight from one end to the other to keep the plane in trim.

After Willoughby's death, his manager, Pyke, was left to clear things up and subsequently we heard no more of the company which had rented the area from us and built the aircraft. The death of Olley cast a gloom over everything but Jane Macdonald did a wonderful job in keeping the place going and we continued CAG training; in fact this was accelerated until the outbreak of war in September. I cannot remember much about this period or any details of the staff we brought in to help but this is probably because I was very fully occupied in other ways.

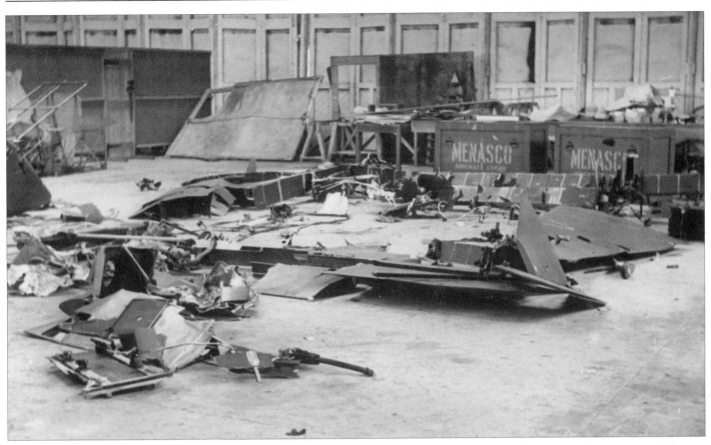

The wreckage of the Willoughby Delta was brought back to Witney and spread out in the hangar. In the lower view the two engines, Menasco Pirate C.4 4-cylinder air-cooled inline inverted piston engines developing125 hp each can be seen.

A complete blackout was enforced

Although war was not unexpected, when it came there was something of an anticlimax; it had little immediate effect on some things but, as far as I was concerned, events moved very rapidly. I was in Church on the Sunday morning when commencement of hostilities was announced. In the afternoon I went to Brize Norton to arrange with some of the men to do ARP work instead of their normal site duties.

The next morning I visited Sandford St. Martin where we were working at the house of Sir Geoffrey Peto who was Regional Controller of the Southern Counties. We had been working there for some time with Thomas Rayson as his architect. Soon after the commencement of the work Sir Geoffrey asked to see me and enquired if I thought I could complete the work without the architect; he thought that this would save time and he paid Rayson's fees and left all the decisions to me! I never saw him again but I saw Lady Peto quite often and we managed to finish the work in the first few weeks of the war.

Another job in progress at this time was at the Blacklock Hotel at Banbury. Here the building, which was roofed in and plastered, was requisitioned and we were asked to store a great many of the fittings such as lifts and an Aga and adapt the building for housing troops. We were working here when Banbury Station was bombed but we escaped without any serious damage.

All activities at the aerodrome were immediately stopped, the aircraft requisitioned and flown to Brize Norton; we were left with the liability of the lease for the remainder of the period. Fortunately we were able to negotiate an arrangement with the de Havilland Aircraft Company to take over the premises and the airfield as a repair depot. They bought all of our equipment, the lease was assigned to them and they sent an advance party under a manager called Thom to take over on September 15th. I forget exactly when petrol was rationed but there was a large stock, nearly 1,000 gallons, in our tanks and I arranged with de Havilland that we could draw on this for the use of Bartlett Brothers. Benge moved his office to a room I had in Gloucester Place where he tied up most of the loose ends; he left to join up on 7th October. The office was retained for some years and long after it was known as 'the aerodrome office'.

Immediately de Havillands took over, Bartlett Brothers started on alterations and additions to the buildings at Witney Aerodrome; this association with de Havillands and later through the Ministry of Aircraft Production, was maintained without a break during the war years. Urgent work on the hangar and ancillary buildings was undertaken, mains electricity brought in, a heating system installed with a new boiler house and chimney. The college was adapted for use as offices and by the end of December we had started on the foundations of two new hangars.

In the meantime we were busy providing accommodation for the army; a hutted camp was built west of the aerodrome and huts for Royal Engineers were being built at Bampton where, in spite of great difficulties with timber licences, several were occupied by the end of the year. There was much urgent work at the Corn Exchange and Drill Hall buildings as well as ARP work in the town; the joiners' shop was working flat out including Saturdays and Sundays.

By the November, H. Gordon Marshall had taken over as general manager at de Havillands. His assistant was Chambers who became a frequent visitor to my home; at his wedding to a girl from Northleigh, we used a float drawn by a grey pony.

During the early months of the war, Witney received a large number of evacuees, amongst these the school from Ashford together with some of the parents and a number of Londoners. Our house was seldom empty – I think we had approximately twenty people who stayed for varying periods over the war years; this, of course, made a lot of extra work for Mary and in addition, amongst other activities, she worked each afternoon at the Red Cross depot on Church Green.

Many stories could be told about the various individuals we had staying with us, some just came and went and were forgotten but several remained as friends, kept in touch and visited us after the war. One of the earliest arrivals, who stayed for any length of time, after the first spate in September, was a Mrs Garner who came with her son from Ashford Grammar School: her husband was serving in the Navy on a destroyer and the first time he came home on leave we offered to put him up. After he arrived the air-raid siren sounded and we had to eat our meal in the dugout because he felt unprotected away from his engine room! The siren had a similar effect on a Captain Morgan who had come straight from Dunkirk; he stayed in bed but insisted on wearing his 'tin hat' until the all-clear sounded. Then there was a girl from the British Council who used her typewriter day and night and a girl from de Havillands whose voice was so raucous that we had to go out to get some relief. There was a surveyor from Scotland who did not stay long, but took most of my cigarettes and tried to leave without paying for his keep; another de Havilland girl always needed me to blow up her bicycle tyres in the morning.

One evacuee we liked very much and often came to see us after the war was Ruth Jones, at one time the secretary to Louis McNiece; she had an unfortunate start – on the evening she arrived Bob Morgan appeared, very drunk and clutching a bottle of gin which he wanted to share. He had been to a party with some of his fellow officers before going back to France. He wanted to spend the evening with us. Ruth married and we lost touch, but another girl, Kay Zimmerman, often stayed with us in later years when we lived at Ash Close, as did the Garners and the Morgans.

Early in the war we employed a man named Foster who had evacuated himself from South London where he had traded as a small builder. We gave him a job in the office and bought up most of his equipment and stock; later he proved himself useful as a small works supervisor particularly as he had a motor cycle and sidecar. However he soon decided to return to London temporarily because the raids had not then started. Another ex-builder who came to us about 1940 was Alfred Timms who was unable to continue trading at Christchurch and had to sell his bungalow down there. We employed him as a wages clerk and he continued with us in a trusted position until he died in harness about 1965. He was liked by everyone and was the most conscientious, trustworthy and likeable employee that I ever had.

In the early months of the war one of the minor occupations was the construction of shelters and for about £50-£75 we produced one in a more or less standard form which was suitable for the average family. The shelters consisted of shuttered concrete sunk in the ground and covered with pre-cast slabs. The whole structure was covered with the excavated soil and provided with a blast protected entrance. There were larger, more elaborate shelters for the public and places of work; these were often built of reinforced Quetta bond brickwork. There were also fire posts and gun pits as well as 'battle headquarters' structures erected at Brize Norton, Rissington, Windrush and other aerodromes. These were quite elaborate undertakings sunk well below ground, waterproofed and plastered and containing all services; we were working on the one at Brize Norton when a stick of bombs destroyed the adjacent hangar.

As soon as war was declared, a complete blackout was enforced. This created a vast amount of minor works in forming light traps and providing other methods for stopping light spillage from buildings; generally wallboard or hardboard was used but later we used vast quantities of cheap quality grey blanket which also served as gas curtains. On moonless nights the complete absence of any light created many problems, not the least of which was the danger of night driving; side and rear lights were almost blacked out and masks fitted to headlights which provided only a small pool of light for about 15 feet (I believe only one headlight was permitted).

Many people were troubled by the darkness but I feel that the problems of those who groped about with the aid of a torch were intensified because the concentrated beam of light prevented the iris in the eye opening as it would in complete darkness. Now there are few places that do not receive some reflected light because of the vast areas provided with illumination but in the past I can recall times of almost complete darkness and I was never ill at ease; there is comfort in the enfolding darkness and I could always find my way in familiar surroundings.

The early part of 1940 was very cold with hard frost that brought the problem of frozen water mains; the supply to 31 Gloucester Place was frozen in the garden. Telephone lines were brought down and branches broken off trees. I found time to go skating at Eynsham but this was the last time that I skated. Unfortunately the photos that I took on that occasion were destroyed with a film that had pictures of the aerodrome on it. In-spite of a snowstorm the troops at Burford Road camp were paraded on the tarmac where we were building the new hangars.

My uncle, William Morley, died and left me £1,000, this was the first legacy I had ever had and I felt very wealthy; for £10 I bought a gold watch which I have kept.

Petrol vouchers and identity cards had been introduced and I had a special pass to let me in to camps and aerodromes but I was seldom stopped or hindered. Cousins had a trailer attached to his car and used it frequently, and overloaded it, because we were always short of transport. In the spring we put in services and built a camp in Marriott's football field. The shelter, in our garden at 31, close by, was constructed completely underground and had bunks and electricity. It was built almost single-handedly by Reg Dore who worked all hours of the day to complete it; fortunately, it was not actually needed for protection but possibly still exists, as might the one built for my mother in the garden of 71 High Street. In later years this became a fine apple store.

Reg Dore was an odd character but I got on well with him and found that he could turn his hand to almost anything. We first employed him 'mossing' stone roofs, he was very agile and quite unaffected by heights; I have seen him carry a heavy ladder up a high roof with perfect balance, quite unsupported by his hands. He never missed an opportunity to help himself and probably did a bit of poaching. We had kept him for some time at the decoy station, which was about a mile from Leafield Radio Station, in order that he could maintain the buildings. One day when I was visiting I found that he was keeping calves in one of the buildings and of course they were enjoying free grazing.

The whole of Leafield Radio Station was camouflaged under heavy netting which gave it the appearance of a hill. During the summer of 1940 we did a great deal of camouflaging, not only at aerodromes but at many factories and mills. It was at Witney that one of the men working on the roof of one of the new hangars was badly injured when he fell about 30 feet; I was always concerned that I might have distracted him by taking off in a Gipsy Moth in order to inspect the camouflaging.

My cousin Jack Bartlett had joined the RAF and when I saw him at Brize Norton where his father (my Uncle Oswald) had rented a cottage, he asked me if I would take charge of some diamonds that he had. We buried them under the concrete floor of the coal house at 31 and retrieved them after the war! We were engrossed with our own affairs and the summer passed by without the momentous events at Dunkirk, the fall of France and the Battle of Britain making any great impression on our day-to-day living. We were concerned, of course we were concerned, but our own affairs seemed little disturbed and the few bombs that fell close by caused no loss of life. Two parachute bombs, the largest we had, came down at Swinbrook (they were probably intended for Leafield Radio Station); one did a lot of damage to roofs and windows. In November, there were two direct hits at Witney, one on Church Green and one at the rear of the brewery but neither hit a building and no one was injured: they were quite small bombs but although we were some distance from where they fell – probably about 1,000 yards – it felt as if they were exploding in our garden. The damage from the blast extended over the whole of Church Green as far as the Market Square and affected a great deal of Corn Street.

Jack Bartlett. *Toni Pull collection*

103

Life became more and more hectic

At the time that the Home Guard was formed, Cousins and I went together to the Police Station with the intention of joining. We were told that we could not be accepted because we were already engaged in other vital activities. Apart from the work we were doing for the Services, we were always on call for demolition. I was in charge of some sort of 'fire post' arrangement in the town and I was also in control of the Emergency Works organisation for the area which enabled me to draw in help in an emergency from a listed number of small builders. Although this was never used, we did obtain help with labour for Witney Aerodrome from Emblings and de Vinney and later on towards the end of the war we drew in Barnes. Jack Barnes was in charge of a gang that was sent to London during the extensive 'doodle bug' damage; it was a joint undertaking and we lost a great deal of plant that was never recovered.

In the early years of the war, life became more and more hectic; we were working long hours each and every day including weekends. It was the rule rather than the exception for some men to be working all day Saturday and Sunday to 4 p.m., sometimes later, and as either Cousins or I had to be there we got little relief.

Gordon Marshall still remained in overall charge at de Havillands but he acquired a right-hand man named Lionel Ward who was a real 'live wire'. Our association became very close and I had great admiration for his ability to get things done and overcome obstacles. I sat in on many of their works conferences with all the heads of production and we had frequent meetings with all those concerned with the building programmes. Many, many times Cousins and I met at Ward's house in the evenings when discussions went on until after midnight. Many times we also accompanied Ward to London for discussions about our programme at the Ministry of Aircraft Production. We also went to Hatfield when the Mosquito project was started there. All this was very wearing; I often flagged but Ward seemed to take it all without visible effect.

As well as the fierce programme at the aerodrome, we were extending and adapting another factory at Charlbury and working on Walker's mill in the Crofts which de Havillands had taken over. Later on Ward had an assistant called Johnstone, who was assisted by Reeves, as a sort of Clerk of Works. Johnstone was an ex-army Captain without much technical knowledge and I never got on well with him; I don't think Ward did either!

Although the work at de Havillands was probably the largest individual job at the time, there was a great deal of other work going on which created problems of supervision and power. Looking back, I wonder how we managed to cope with it all. We were involved with War Office (WO) camps at Ramsden Heath, Great Missenden, Shurlock Row, Adlestrop and Bradwell Grove and others. There was much factory work at Integral Equipment, Crawford Colletts, the local mills, Cirencester and Tetbury, with work also at food stores, ammunition stores, and direction-finding stations. In the area, we also provided concrete bases for pylons for new lines run by the Central Electricity Board and many other activities too numerous to mention. There was also a need for meetings to coordinate projects, for example Works committees, foremen's meetings, manpower meetings and meetings for the group leaders of Fire Guard Posts. I spent considerable time at Oxford with Cannon and Giles of the Federation and with Walker and Hinkins in connection with the Southern Builder's Emergency Organisation. I had also to keep in touch with the leaders of the local builders' emergency organisation such as Hill at Eynsham, Toly at Bladon, Pether at Burford, Green at Bampton amongst others. All this took time.

The availability and deferment of men was always with us and a great deal of building labour was directed into factories. The manager of the local Ministry of Labour Office, Percy Brunt, was always prepared to cut 'red tape' when it was really necessary and I got on well with him.

I was also involved with ARP meetings and once went to Bristol on a tour of inspection after some heavy raids so that I could see how they coped with fire damage.

In spite of all the above we did manage to get some work done in the yard. The large garage that started life as a barn, was made into a store with a raised floor for loading cement at lorry bed level and a range of four garages and a workshop were built at right angles to it; this structure had a flat concrete roof which could be used for additional storage space. The tall chimney that had been built about 1880 to a height of 84 feet was showing signs of becoming unsafe so we employed some steeplejacks to ladder it and we decided to demolish the upper portion down to a height of about 50 feet: brickwork was thrown down the inside of the shaft and cleared away from the base. The lightning conductor was re-fixed and later on the stack was banded.

Barry Taylor climbing the chimney in Bartlett's Yard.

The chimney in a corner of the Yard.

As time went on both Cousins and I began to feel the need for a break and towards the end of 1941 I went with John Welch to Amberley for a few days. Cousins began to get away to Cheltenham or Cardiff where his sister lived. I think we both realised that unless we had some relaxation we would be unable to maintain an efficient standard of work. Cousins worked far longer hours than I did and got through more work. Although the year's turnover eventually reached over £43,000 in 1941, it fell over the remaining years of the war but the effort required to cope with all the difficulties and frustrations which abounded was still great.

We were involved in quite a lot of farm work, some under the direction of the War Agricultural Committee and other work that comes to mind was in relation to the Prisoner of War (POW) camp at Milton, development at Enstone Airfield and the joint sewage scheme for the Burford Road camp and de Havillands.

About 1943, I relinquished control of the Fire Guards organisation and Cousins took over the main areas of the town; this he organised more efficiently than I ever did but I still took my turn on the rota of night duty.

My Uncle Percy acquired a brown pony called Stella, which he used in a tub when he went shooting. Fred Jones, who worked for him in the sausage factory, looked after the pony and drove him. Stella was kept in a stable that I had made and grazed in the Close with Uncle Joe's permission. She was far from docile and really unsuitable for driving and I started to ride her. Uncle Percy was crippled with arthritis but he continued to enjoy shooting; I made him a chair mounted on a ball race so that he could swing round to anything driven to him and he was still an excellent shot. When he bought another small grey pony, which did everything he wanted, I made him a float mounted on pneumatic tyres and this proved successful. Stella was really too small for me, but as I

About this time the back wing of the house where my mother lived, No. 71, was altered to form a cottage containing a living room, kitchen, and WC on the ground floor, with two bedrooms over. At the same time the opposite wing which had been a woodshed was made into an additional small kitchen for my mother's use; she then had three other people living in the house.

My Uncle Ern was then living with his brother Joe at No. 75. He made frequent trips to Liverpool where he had an interest in a fuse-making firm, the Bulwark Fuse Company, run by his partner Albion; the factory was hit several times in the raids and was eventually demolished.

A. J. Timms lived in the cottage and we continued to find him a valuable addition to the staff. With the help of the clerk, Miss Barnes, who had been with us since about 1936, Cousins and I coped with all the administration work throughout the early part of the war; we had lost Johnson, the clerk who was called up at the outbreak. Foster had helped and we had a boy Basson (and later John Baston). Timms was excellent in every way and we were getting through well over £40,000 of work in the year. Sometime in 1942 we had help from a builder, Wyatt, from Marston, however he fell short of our expectations when we started Bradwell Grove Hospital in 1943. Here we had a site office and employed de Vinney as agent and it was here that Adams started as a wages clerk; later he came into the office in Witney where he worked well with Timms and remained with us for many years after the war.

Percy Bartlett with his custom-made chair, with the seat mounted on a ball race.

The ball race built into the base of the chair.

enjoyed riding and with the help of Fred Jones, I tried out one or two other horses. Eventually I bought a mare called Mona Bridges which I rode for years.

We had no difficulty in riding through the outskirts of the town which, in those days, was quiet with little traffic on the roads. Adjacent to Early's mill was a track that led to the river and on to Crawley, Minster Lovell, and also to Hailey and Singe Wood. From the New Yatt Road a bridleway led to Raymond Blake's Farm where I was always welcome; in fact we could travel over a large area of countryside away from roads and traffic without hindrance.

I rented some fields at the rear of Viners, east of the High Street, where the horses could easily be turned out and we had the Close and some boxes at the top of the yard. Fred Jones became a friend and a very loyal servant; he always looked after my horses and came to work for me full time after Uncle Percy sold his business to Brazils. Fred constructed the new garden and surroundings when we built Ash Close and looked after the horses, the cow and all the other livestock. He had served in the cavalry throughout the First World War and later for some years in Egypt. I shall always be grateful to him for all that he taught, for his devotion and absolute reliability. Those like him belong to a world gone by.

It was during these war years that Mary fell and injured both of her knees. In spite of two sessions and operations in the Wingfield Hospital, these injuries became an increasing handicap with arthritis, restriction of movement and continuous pain. With great courage she continued, as far as it was possible, to lead and enjoy a normal life.

Fred Jones with Percy's new pony and trap in front of Cape Terrace in Gloucester Place, Witney.

Percy's alternative mode of transport.

Percy's earlier mode of transport, a de Dion motor tricycle. This was one of three owned by Oswald, Christopher and Percy.

Barry and Mona Bridges with a fine portrait of Mona Bridges inset.

Barry and Fred Jones haymaking.

Mary with Haze, the Jersey cow.

Apple picking time.

The immediate post-war years produced a heyday of activity

Over this period, the annual turnover from the business had remained at about £30,000/£35,000 and I was still trading as an individual. In 1944 we considered forming a limited liability company and in March 1945 this came into being as Bartlett Bros. (Witney) Ltd; I passed over all assets (about £5,000) in return for shares. With my appointment as Chairman and governing director I was allotted 198 ordinary shares, John Welch (as company secretary) one share, Cousins one share and I held all the preference shares. It was not until 1949 that the name of the company was changed to Bartlett Brothers Ltd.

When I had negotiated the lease of the yard in 1931, Moody advised me to have a clause inserted which gave me an option to purchase the property at any time during the 14 year term of the lease for the sum of £3,000. At that time this figure was considered to be a top value for the property, including the house. I do not think my uncle considered it likely that I should be in a position to exercise the option in his lifetime but in March 1945 it became obvious that I must avail myself of the option before it expired; he was naturally concerned that it included the house that he was

living in. When I gave him the licence to occupy the house for his life, I think he was really quite happy and content with the arrangement. In the meantime other options had been agreed with him at values that had been independently approved and which I had no intention of exercising during his lifetime; I think he was relieved that all the property was available to me if I was able to purchase it. These other options to purchase were on the garden and orchard together with the back land to the west, including the buildings of the old generating station and garages in Gloucester Place for £1,750, the shop and flat known as 73 High Street for £1,650 and the house known as 71 High Street for £1,100.

BARTLETT BROTHERS
LIMITED

BUILDING ⅋ CONTRACTORS

WITNEY
OXON

DIRECTORS:
E. BARTLETT TAYLOR
J. E. COUSINS
J. W. WELCH
C. DRIVER
J. DINGLE

TELEPHONE:
WITNEY 84

Headed note paper for Bartlett Brothers Limited 1949.

After purchasing the yard in 1945, I rented the old generating station from my uncle; he was pleased to see this made into a joiners' shop with modern machines installed. He also lived to see the start of the new house being built at the end of the yard; he had willingly agreed to give up a portion of his garden so that the new dwelling could be built over the boundary. After he died in 1946, the wisdom of agreeing these options to purchase the properties which surrounded the yard became apparent. At the time that I made these arrangements, I was not farsighted enough to appreciate this. As one of my uncle's trustees, it would have been

difficult for me to purchase these freeholds without establishing some assurance that the estate was receiving the best possible price for them and this might have necessitated a sale by auction.

I have sometimes regretted that I was not able to purchase some of the other freeholds in his estate. However, at the time, I did my best to negotiate the best possible sales of these and it was not possible to see into the future. One pair of Close houses was sold by private treaty for £4,000, the adjoining pair, similar in all respects, went for £2,500 at auction. The remaining land and buildings on the west of the road to Curbridge (about 10 acres and 20 buildings)

The improved joiners' shop with Jack Lock (left) and Peter Franklin (right) in 1945. Below are two views of the shop with machinery installed.

Above: Further extensions to the joinery in 1949.

Left and below: Views of the Yard 1949. In the lower view the houses of Gloucester Place can be seen in the background.

was sold for £7,000 and the remainder on the main aerodrome for £3,250; both more than I would have been prepared to pay myself. These areas have now become extremely valuable industrial sites and would have been a good investment.

The immediate post-war years produced a heyday of activity. There was a gradual increase in turnover and we were making preparations for expansion but there were still many restrictions that made any private building difficult. Building licences were still required and timber licences were difficult to get. Fortunately we maintained quite a volume of 'essential' work which helped to ease the situation when we were asked to undertake some private building.

The last year of my trading as an individual ended in March 1945 with a turnover of about £30,000; as a company, in 1946 this was £32,000, increasing to £50,000 and £65,000 in 1947 and 1948. In 1946 the shares I held in Bartlett Bros. Ltd amounted to £7,600 (Cousins held £1,400) and around this time I also made other investments. The freehold of the yard had cost £3,000 and during the war I had paid my mother £1,000 for the house at Wimbledon. She was anxious to pass over the responsibilities of maintaining and letting it but she still received the income from it and I also provided her some additional income from the business.

In 1945 I purchased two cottages at South Leigh, one was occupied by Charles Bryan, his niece, Nancy Penson, and her mother. When their cottage came up for auction, they were afraid of being turned out so I bought it and the adjoining one; I'm not sure now if I paid £500 for the two or £500 each! The rent I received was only nominal but, like all property then, it was an appreciating asset; it was my good fortune to be able to acquire it.

Unfortunately I did not retain the house at Wimbledon for very long. In 1941 my mother had found a tenant named Pepperall who was then head of the Milk Marketing Board at Thames Ditton. He paid £80 per year and proved an excellent tenant; he became a personal friend of mine and I used to dine with him in Town. When he died at the end of 1953, I decided to sell the house, while it was vacant; I could not contemplate re-letting it. Unfortunately at that time the house market was at a low ebb and it only made around £3,000. It was a costly mistake.

In the latter part of 1945 I got involved with a man called Maple and we ran a small grocery shop at Langford. He proved to be an unstable character and in a short time we sold the business: I retrieved my capital and he went to Hove, so my experience of the grocery trade was short-lived. Another unsuccessful venture about this time was my involvement in a scheme to open a pub at Arncott, near Bicester. Bill Deeley owned a farmhouse at Wood Farm, which was near the Ordnance Depot and he, Percy Collett and I got together. We purchased a property for £1,600 and obtained a licence to open as a pub which we called the Tally Ho! Unfortunately Percy Collett got cold feet and backed out; as he was going to run it, we had no option but to give up the idea and we sold it, with the licence, to Clinch's Brewery for about what it cost. This could have proved a very successful venture in view of the development of the adjoining depot and it was a bad decision; the Tally Ho! is still running as a thriving pub, owned by Courage who were Clinch's successors.

I had also bought some land north of the main Burford Road, opposite the Water Tower. This was a triangular site with a lot of road frontage but the ground fell away steeply from the road; later when we were building a new factory for Smiths of England, we tipped hundreds of loads of excavated material to raise the level. In the fifties it was sold to Clinchs, again as a pub site but when they built the Windrush pub, a fraction nearer the town, the land was not used. Another site I bought on the Woodstock Road, adjacent to Northfield Farm entrance, was used as a tip for all the excavated material from the new school we built on neighbouring land. The site was later sold and we built on it a meeting hall and a bungalow.

After the war, Witney Aerodrome Ltd and the club had a surplus of funds which we decided to invest in the block of land and eight houses known as Leys Villas when this property came on the market. I believe the total cost was £6,500 or £7,000; when we sold

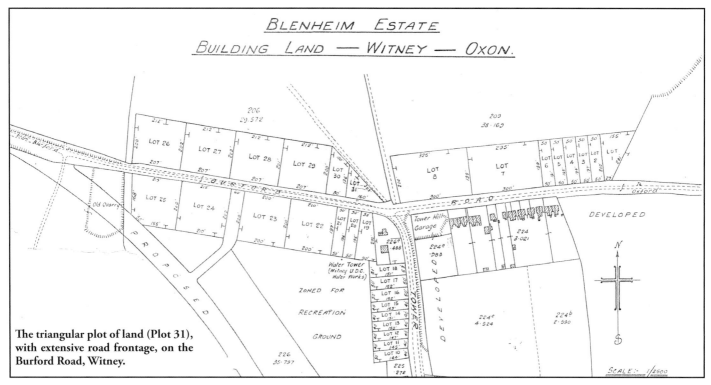

The triangular plot of land (Plot 31), with extensive road frontage, on the Burford Road, Witney.

Preparing the site for the building of 'Woodstock Road School'. All three views look towards Woodstock Road.

Below: The completed school was called Wood Green and is seen here from the rear looking towards Woodstock Road.

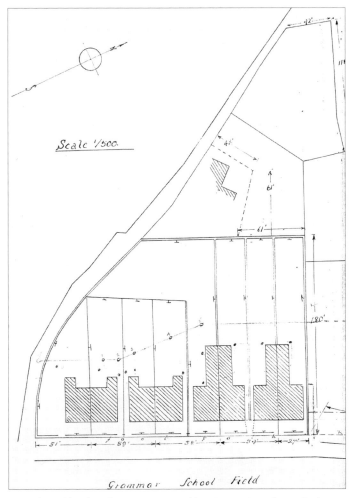

Plan of land and property owned by Witney Aerodrome Ltd.

Two views of Ash Close.

one house this ran us into trouble with the Inland Revenue who said we were trading in houses. However we eventually convinced them that it was only one transaction and we paid no tax. The companies were wound up and the unsold houses were divided between Jane MacDonald and myself. The back land was bought by me, I can't remember what I paid for it probably about £500.

As mentioned earlier my uncle died in July 1946 and this involved me in a lot of activity in clearing up his estate. There was much correspondence and many negotiations concerning the sale of the various properties and in the end the estate was wound up leaving only one house, 31 Gloucester Place unsold. In time, this was occupied by Uncle Ern and was retained until his wife moved into a home in 1965. When Uncle Joe's estate was finally cleared up the five legatees benefited to the extent of nearly £5,000 each in addition to specific legacies amounting to about £1,200.

At the same time I was busily engaged in the building of our new house which we had decided to name Ash Close because it was built on the land at the rear of the yard shown in the earliest deeds as Ashfield's Close. Although it was started in the summer of 1946 and roofed in by the end of the year, progress was hampered by the exceptional winter weather which closed in after Christmas 1946. It was the worst winter I can remember with almost unbroken snow and ice to the end of March 1947. Almost all outside building work came to a standstill and what was undercover was carried out with great difficulty; there were a great many labour problems and altogether it was a disastrous winter for the building trade. In

spite of all this we moved into the new house early in April; soon afterwards we experienced a severe gale which blew down the big ash tree in the field. Fred Jones was an invaluable help at this time and as well as his other areas of work, new boxes for the horses were built and we grassed down the old vegetable garden as an extension to the paddock.

Part of the house at 75, where my uncle had lived, was made into offices which gave us the much needed extra accommodation in the form of a reception area, general office and my own office on the ground floor. Our original office on the first floor, which had been used for almost everything, was designated as the wages office. Cousins had part of the first floor and two other rooms were used by surveyors. Fred Jones went to live in the front of the old house where he had two ground floor rooms, two bedrooms and a kitchen.

About this time Austin Moody died and we had to find another accountant; Moody had advised and helped me for nearly twenty years and I knew I should miss him, however Brazils introduced me to their accountants, who had an office at Dunstable, and Leonard Turquand took over our affairs.

Ernest Bartlett Taylor's office on the ground floor of 75 High Street.

The office of Jim Cousins on the first floor of 75 High Street.

A glimpse through the doorways.

The accounts office, home of Mr Timms.

Witney began to expand

My mother was still living at 71 and Lily Howitt, my father's cousin, came from Wigston to live with her. Alf Timms and his wife moved from the cottage at the back of the house and for a short time this was let to the postmaster; later Miss Tanner moved into it and lived there until my mother died. The house at Wigston where Lily Howitt had lived was left to Harvey Madeley by his uncle; when Lily left he was able to sell it and generously supplied Lily with a sum of money from the proceeds; after this she was able to buy an annuity, that I arranged on her behalf. Mother died at the end of 1948 and Lily and Miss Tanner lived in the house at 71 and

paid me a small rent until it was turned into an Abbeyfield Home.

About 1950 I tried to buy the old barn that backed onto the garden on 71; this had been acquired by Jordan the blacksmith and I made an offer for the whole premises known as 67 High Street. He decided, however, to retain it for his own use and we agreed to pull down the top of the barn and make it into a workshop, after building up the windows overlooking the garden. I also tried to buy 77 High Street, adjoining the yard, after Miss Andrews died in 1950 but it was put up for auction and I had to pay £3,850 for it in 1951. Mr Tanner, Mary's father, died in 1951 and Chestnuts was sold; Mary did not wish me to buy it.

71 High Street which became an Abbeyfield Home.

At this time, we developed the back land at the Leys; this I had acquired from the Aerodrome Company; at the same time we provided a main sewer for all the existing Leys houses. On the land we built nine or ten houses and seven garages and put in a road from the Springs. In the same year we formed the company known as Rolyat Plant Ltd to handle all the plant and machines and engaged a manager, Hodges, who lived at 77. My cousin Denis Bartlett was engaged as a safety officer which gave him a small income and helped with his car running expenses.

Barry with his mother, Caroline.

Right: **Bill Thurston at the development at the Springs in Witney with the garages in the right background.**

Below: **A letterhead for Rolyat Plant Ltd.**

ROLYAT PLANT LTD.

PLANT HIRE CONTRACTORS,
BUILDERS' EQUIPMENT

Directors:
M. E. TAYLOR
E. B. TAYLOR

TELEPHONE : WITNEY 84

75 HIGH STREET,
WITNEY,
OXON.

Above & right: **The development at Spring Close.**

My uncles, Ern and Oswald, seemed anxious to invest some money in the business for which I paid rather more interest than they would obtain elsewhere. Actually I did not, at that time, need capital and I let a number of other people have money on loan at a lower rate!

In 1952 I bought Farm Mill from the Duke of Marlborough for about £1,300. As far as I can remember this came about after my friend Walter Hewitt had given up his business as a corn merchant; he had retired because of ill-health but after the lapse of time I am a little vague about the details. He had rented the mill from the Duke and used it as a store. The water-wheel, gearing and shafting were all in working order and he employed a man called Pickett to run it for grinding; Pickett lived in a cottage attached to the mill. The Duke was prepared to sell the mill to Walter Hewitt and in the event it was agreed that I should buy it. The purchase included the mill and cottage, all the land (about 3½ acres) on the north, bordering the leat stream together with about 4 acres of allotment land on the south, the osier beds and all the roadways and streams.

In 1953 I sold the mill and the land on the north to Maclean, who had a market garden at Kingston Bagpuize, for £2,200 and I think he let it to Pickett's son John who tried unsuccessfully to run

a small corn shop. Later I was able to help his wife with a loan so that they could retain their house in the Crofts. On the sale of the mill, there was a net gain of about £778 after expenses and this I handed over to Hilda Hewitt as by this time Walter was very ill. This left me with the remaining land which had cost me nothing but at the time seemed of little value. We made use of the area of osier beds as a store after raising the level. With hindsight of course the mill buildings should have been retained; they could have been converted into a house in delightful surroundings which would have been much sought after but at the time the site seemed of little value.

I also purchased land called The Moors from Crawford Colletts for £1,250. This came about after a casual conversation at a meeting on the future of their factory with their directors (Linzell, Eve, Miss Emms), Cousins and I. They had purchased the land with the intention of building a new factory but ran into planning difficulties and decided to build on their own site near the old workhouse. The Moors, an area of about 10 acres, had been glebe land belonging to Cogges Church. At the time I did not look on it as having much value and I really bought it with the idea of using it for grazing as it was near to the Close via Puck Lane. Quite soon,

The house built at the Leys for Barry's cousin Molly Lomas.

Witney began to expand and a new road (Welch Way) was being considered. The Urban District Council was already making plans for more housing and I was unable to prevent them taking about 3.8 acres of the best of the land that I had bought. By July 1954 they had acquired the land, with its value assessed at £275; in the end I managed to get another £760 for loss of land development value. At this time I had money invested in several mortgages and I was able to help Cousins purchase some property and land at Carterton which later he was able to develop profitably.

In 1954 John Welch was instrumental in arranging an agreement with a Nurse Francis at Northleigh. This was that I would pay her £1,500 for the bungalow that she lived in and allow her to occupy it for her lifetime. After Nurse Francis died, I sold some of the land to the Rural District Council for housing and gave the bungalow to my cousin Molly Lomas to add to her income; later on, I also let Molly have the seven garages that we had built at Spring Close.

Early in 1955 Bartlett Brothers bought 79 High Street for £6,000. This completed the block of property, with High Street frontage, from Long's shop to Gloucester Place. I already owned all the back-land as far as Puck Lane with the exception of the area of the Close on which the six Gloucester Place houses were built; No. 79 became vacant when my Uncle Percy's widow, Blanche, died and when negotiating the price, I was keen to ensure I was being fair to my cousins.

Blanche Bartlett at 'Moorside', 79 High Street.

At this time I was offered £4,000 worth of shares in Marriott's mill; this was about four times their par value on which they were paying 40%, but I am glad to say I did not buy them, although I might have gained some benefit when they amalgamated with Earlys. I tried to negotiate with Dominey, who looked after Marriott's affairs, to purchase the field used by Witney football club and the neighbouring garden, on which the gazebo was built, all of which adjoined my property. He intimated that they were prepared to sell when I offered £1,000 for the field and £250 for the garden, but procrastinated by referring back to the 'family' and nothing ever came of it.

The affairs of Bartlett Brothers were prospering, turnover had built up after the war and by 1950 had reached £70,000. We were carrying out a lot of industrial work. In addition to all the new development at Smiths of England, we built a new factory for Crawford Colletts and added considerably to the Witney Blanket Company's factory; later we rebuilt the whole factory after a disastrous fire. There continued to be much work at the blanket mills, other industries and at schools and public buildings. By 1953 turnover

reached £125,000 and by 1956 it was nearly £200,000. Both Cousins and I enjoyed the active business life and the personal association we had with all the work going on but we felt we needed some help.

In 1955, Driver was engaged as an assistant manager; Hodges had left. Aucutt came the same year and took charge of the Rolyat books. We engaged another general foreman, C. Barber, who moved into the house at 77, while Driver moved into 79. Charles Day was already looking after the work on Smith's site with Frank Buckingham as general foreman. At this time I renewed the contact with Gardner & Theobald who were the quantity surveyors

Right: **Charles Monk and the low loader and mortar mixer c. 1950.**

Vehicles in Barlett's Yard c 1950.

119

Digging the sewer at Smiths of England in 1957 – distance 2,300 yards, maximum depth 19 feet.

Below: Ted Maycock on the site at Smiths of England.

The area around Smiths of England. The picture was taken from their new office block.

employed on the construction of the new factory for Smiths of England under Sir Thomas Bennett; we carried out several million pounds worth of work in a most harmonious atmosphere. John Cannell, who had been with Garner & Theobald for some time, was made a partner and my association with him continued long after John Theobald's death.

The increased office staff consisted of J. Dingle, Timms, Adams, Aucutt, Miss Mayo and a boy. With this staff, helped by a supervisor Charles French, and four general foremen, Cousins and I ran the business, I think, efficiently. In 1958 we carried out £381,000 worth of work showing a gross profit of £35,000 with a net return of over £8,000. The profit on the plant hire by Rolyat amounted to £3,300 on a turnover of £13,000 for the year.

By the middle of the 1950s, I had built up considerable personal capital – in addition to the money invested in Bartlett Brothers Ltd, and in the High Street properties (71, 73, 75, 77 and 79), the back land and Ash Close, I had acquired a number of other investments. Two houses in Leys Villas, two houses at Hailey and two cottages at South Leigh were tenanted and I held mortgages on several freeholds. I had also made various short term loans to individuals, mostly secured by property. It was sometime before I realised that mortgages and loans were an unsatisfactory form of investment; they produced income that I did not really need and the capital was neither appreciating nor easily realised. I would have been far better employed in the purchase of land and property but I did not know this at the time. There had been many occasions when I could have bought properties if only I had chosen to increase my offers. It is equally obvious that I should have retained certain properties, but some showed me a fair profit whilst others served their purpose in helping other people.

Bartlett's office staff 1950 left to right: A. J. Timms, C. Day, Miss Mayo, J. Dingle and L. Adams.

In 1956 I negotiated the purchase of some land at the rear of 150 Newland which consisted of about 6 or 7 acres belonging to the Church Commissioners; this area had been leased to the Urban District Council who no longer required it. Negotiations with the valuers went on from August 1956 and eventually, in November 1957 it was acquired for £1,435; this included the electricity substation for which the Board paid rent. All this area adjoined the frontage owned by Tom Smith who lived in the house and ran a small joinery works. He had worked for us as a joiner and obviously it was a valuable asset for him to acquire. I had always been on good terms with him, so it was bought in his name and he was given a loan to pay for it.

Further expansion in the joinery August 1955.

In the spring of 1957, I had another fight with the Urban District Council who were still trying to obtain the remainder of the land known as the Moors. The new road from High Street to the junction of Tower Hill, Curbridge Road, Ducklington Lane and Corn Street had been approved and although the line of the road did not go through my land, it bordered it. They had already taken ground for the car park and land to the west for housing together with land for a road from Dark Lane. I could see no reason why they should have the remainder.

By the end of 1957 we had decided that the amount of industrial work being undertaken by Bartlett Brothers could be dealt with more efficiently by forming a separate company; this provided certain tax advantages and a safeguard if things went wrong. In the spring of 1958 Bartlett Brothers Industrial Ltd came into being.

We did not visualise such rapid growth

In July 1958 Crawley Farm was auctioned and I bought about 170 acres of land together with the farmhouse, farm buildings in the village and two cottages for £9,500. The first thing was to convert some of the buildings into dwellings; Sally, the daughter of my cousin Phyllis, and her husband Peter Waas lived in the old farmhouse until one of these was ready. The two cottages and later the farmhouse and another barn were sold off and a new set of buildings for milking, livestock and storage was erected in Broken Hatch Lane. The stream that ran right through the land was dredged, part was diverted and some land exchanged with Clinch's Brewery. As time went by more adjoining land was bought and much later a new house was built at Broken Hatch and all the converted buildings sold off. The size of the farm eventually reached a total of over 300 acres, with a tenancy of a further 50 acres or so. This together with the house and farm buildings was sold in 1978 by Sally and Peter for over £475,000.

In the early part of 1959 I was incapacitated with sciatica and for some weeks I was unable to get about. This came at a difficult time because it had been agreed that Fred Jones should retire and I was trying to find someone to take his place. I bought 27 West End (for £1,100) for him to live in and he continued to look after the pony. I employed an ex-policeman named Blake to look after the garden and milk the cow and he took up residence in 75 High Street. However Blake did not last long, he left in the spring of 1960. I replaced him with Howells, who had been a cowman with Jeffries at South Leigh. He seemed able to look after the cow and pony and had some knowledge of gardening but we soon found that he lacked the personal concern that Jones had had for his work. In the early days of his retirement, Jones enjoyed exercising the pony and frequently came to see us but unfortunately he soon became less active and died at his home in West End in 1963. During 1963

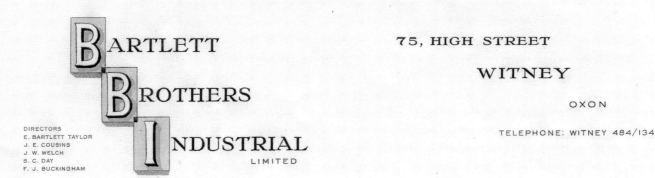

Notepaper headings Bartlett Brothers Limited and the new Bartlett Brothers Industrial Limited which was formed in 1958.

Howells spent long periods at home unwell. Frequently I had to get someone to do his work and milk the cow. I shall always be grateful to Bert Pratley who was always ready to come at short notice and who still came to help at apple picking until he died in 1976. Howells moved out of the house No. 75 in 1974 and Howe came to work with us in February that year. Both Haze, the cow, and Judy, the pony, had been put down while Howells was in charge so there was no livestock except for a few hens.

Following the death of Uncle Christopher, I became concerned about affairs at Sandford Mount in Charlbury; the house had been the home of his family, Denis, Phyllis and Bernard, for many years. I had helped him in the past but now the estate was weighed down with liabilities and I wondered what would happen when it had to be sold, as it seemed it would have to be. With an early sale the family would at least be free from debt and have some capital. After the sale of the property, Peter Burchett, Phyllis's son-in-law was able to buy back the house and precincts for about £7,000 and subsequently it was retained in the family!

During this time I was corresponding with Jack Bartlett about the farm at Stoke Talmage which his mother had owned. I made several journeys, met the tenants in an endeavour to help him with his difficulties and managed to find someone prepared to buy it. I was taken aback when he then sold it by auction for very little money.

In the spring of 1960 we were considering a complete re-organisation of finances. The Industrial Company had been formed and was undertaking a lot of work, Rolyat Plant was serving its purpose but a great deal of money was locked up in Bartlett Brothers Ltd, the original company, who also owned freeholds totalling about £25,000. It was decided to liquidate this company, which we had formed in 1945 and form two new companies – Bartlett Brothers (1960) Ltd and Bartlett's Joinery Ltd. As far as I can remember the total assets were just under £100,000 and after expenses, the balance was shared between me, Cousins and John Welch in proportion to our share holdings – 9,000, 1,500 and 250 respectively. I took the houses at Hailey and the Leys garages at about £3,800, John Welch took the Spring Close house at £1,700. The freeholds of the yard and 79 High Street were passed to Bartlett Brothers Industrial for £19,250; I had sold the yard to the company in 1958 for £12,500 and they had purchased No. 79 for £6,000 in 1955. Bartlett Brothers Industrial was already under capitalised and the acquisition of these freeholds had to be supported by a mortgage. This had to be registered against the company and of course reflected on their credit. It was a mistake.

Most of the capital for the new companies was provided by me, Cousins and John Welch – Day and Buckingham had shares in Bartlett Brothers Industrial Ltd and Driver and Dingle, in Bartlett

Barry's Uncle Christopher, with some of his bee hives.

Sandford Mount, Charlbury (1920). This house was, for many years, Christopher's home.   *Kate Bradley collection*

Brothers 1960 Ltd. Mary held nearly all the shares in Rolyat Plant and Cousins, John Welch, and I held all those in Bartlett's Joinery. Looking back I am not sure now if we were right or wrong in what we did – as individuals we protected our own capital (mostly mine) and to a large extent we avoided payment of profits tax by distributing large amounts of the profits but crucially the companies were increasingly short of capital as they grew. Had they remained static in turnover, I think our ideas were sensible but we did not visualise such rapid growth.

At the end of 1960, when we had nearly completed the winding-up, Cousins wrote me a note setting out the reasons for his concern as to what would happen if things went wrong with Bartlett Brothers Industrial. He said that they were now "flying pretty high and wide", turnover had reached about £350,000 and although our financial interests were so far secured they could be jeopardised by "passing over freeholds without proper safeguards". He pointed out that in addition to normal trade creditors, the company had liabilities of nearly £24,000 on an issued capital of about £10,000. However Bartlett Brothers Industrial and the other companies continued to thrive and make good profits but we both wanted to reduce our responsibilities. The strain over the years was beginning to tell on our drive and energy and we were anxious to pass over more responsibility to the younger directors. We reluctantly decided, however, that the amount of turnover which must be maintained might be more than they could handle without help and guidance and that it would also become difficult to maintain standards. Early in 1961 Cousins became unwell and had a spell in the Masonic Hospital at Chiswick; he still kept in touch with things and was back in harness again in April.

Following on after the war, I still continued active participation in the affairs of the Federation. In the fifties I was asked to consider being president of the Oxfordshire Federation but decided that it would be too time consuming and refused. I still gave considerable time to their affairs including serving on the Appeals Tribunal which sat in Oxford quite frequently.

I was also involved with various educational bodies and as a governor of the West Oxfordshire Technical College from its inception. I saw it grow under two principals but began to disagree with some of the policies and eventually resigned. For a great many years I was governor of the Witney Educational Foundation which included, amongst its trusts and freeholds, the original Witney Grammar School building and several areas of land and vested in it was the original Holloway's Charity and Wright's gift. In the early days it did little more than provide money to assist in the payment of apprenticeship premiums for boys to learn a trade but later a considerable sum became available each year and the scope of assistance was widened. This came about after the sale of an area of land adjoining the Woodstock Road which is now covered by Early Road and its surroundings. As a representative of this Foundation, I was also appointed to the Board of Governors of Witney Grammar School and as a governor I attended the luncheon and met the Queen Mother on the occasion of her visit during the tercentenary celebration in 1960.

In the same year, 1960, we started a branch of the Abbeyfield Society in Witney. I let them have the old house at 71 High Street as a home. After alterations had been carried out this provided accommodation for six people and a housekeeper. A little later on I managed to buy two adjoining houses in Corn Street (69 and 71)

Jim Cousins at Witney Trade Fair 1961, with the cup won by Bartlett Brothers for best stand. On the left is Charles Day.

and after considerable alteration these made another suitable home with room for eight people at a net cost of around £7,000; this cost was defrayed almost entirely by a legacy to the Witney Society by the Barton family.

After the return of Cousins from hospital in 1961, we were both taking an active part in the affairs of the various companies but I think we were both inclined to try to leave more to the younger directors and we both had other interests. Cousins had started to develop the land that he had at Carterton. I was concerned in the affairs of Crawley Farm and the Abbeyfield homes and was still purchasing properties such as 127 Corn Street, Park View, Charlbury and another in West End; I still also had considerable capital locked up in mortgages.

In the spring of 1962 I experienced problems with my health and spent two periods in the Radcliffe Hospital and saw several specialists. Since about 1947 I had experienced frequent discomfort and pain and in the spite of specialists, X-rays etc. this persisted. I now think that it was due to nervous tension and the pace of living during the war. Throughout this time I had a very good friend in Dr Tothill of Woodstock and in 1963 I spent several weeks at Champneys, near Tring. The treatment and advice I received there and the later help from naturopaths, osteopaths and chiropractors altered my life. I cannot speak too highly of the results they achieved.

In the 1960s the turnover from the Bartlett Brothers group of companies continued to rise and all the companies were making good profits but in 1962 Cousins expressed a wish to obtain an outside opinion on management efficiency and we agreed to employ some management consultants, Work Simplification Ltd. They spent some time studying our system of operating together with the costs over the past three years and in their report they stressed the advantages of merging the control of the two companies, Bartlett Brothers Industrial and Bartlett Brothers 1960; this they said would avoid cleavage of staff, the duplication of stores and the purchasing of materials. This always was and had been economically obvious to us but we were also aware, much more than they were, that the differing outlooks of Day and Driver would make such a merger difficult. The further suggestion of a 'plan of management' and a job control system, which they offered to undertake at a cost of about £2,000, was at first favoured by Cousins and John Welch but to my mind this was wrapped up with the first suggestion of common control; unless this was possible the rosy picture which might have been created by following their advice was unlikely and I believed that with our own long experience of management we were more aware of the pitfalls. The two companies continued to trade as separate entities under the management of Day and Driver respectively and by March 1963 the total group turnover was well in excess of half a million and showed a profit of some £26,000.

Alf Timms, who had served us so well since he came in 1939, had now grown very old; he had lost his wife and moved into the new flats on Woodgreen with his sister but we had great difficulty in dissuading him from coming conscientiously to the office each day! I had bought the house he lived in and the one adjoining from Miss Mawle and we used these and part of 77 and 79 High Street to house some of the staff.

In 1964 I bought back the yard and 79 from Bartlett Brothers Industrial for £19,250 and was still looking for farmland as an investment to take the place of the mortgages that I held.

We had many adventures with clocks

For some time I had corresponded with people who were interested in the preservation of old tools and equipment. When the new museum was opened at Fletcher's House in Woodstock, I was introduced to the Director, Jean Cook. We had in the yard a number of items that were old enough to be of interest and I presented them to the museum. These items included: a wheelwright's vice, several pit saws and one bottom handle (which is rare), several saw-pit dogs and timber chains, the large flywheel and gearing that drove the wood lathe and lathe tools, several bits and rods for boring wooden water pipes and some boring heads and rods, blacksmith's tools and drill, rope blocks, lewises and stone-lifting gear, some early bottle-type fire extinguishers, hay knives, corn and chaff shovels, a corn sieve, a chaff cutter, a straw bond twister and some straw bee skeps, a lathe tying tool, steelyards, fire dogs, a crane and spit jack (made by Thos. May of Witney). I also let them have Malachi Bartlett's large tool chest and all the tools left in it. I later retrieved the chest for my own use!

About this time, Earlys decided to sell some of their properties including Newland warehouse, New Mills and Farm Mill. I agreed to buy the latter for £3,500; I already owned the surrounding land on the west and the sale of the mill included that at the rear and, so I thought, the mill stream. However we could not agree about the riparian rights and I withdrew; it was, I think, sold to the County Council as a store. At this time we were trying to get planning permission to raise the level of the surrounding land, which I owned, so that it could be used for storage of builders' materials and possibly a joinery works. I had already agreed in principle with Robinson, the Chief Planning Officer, about what we proposed to do but unfortunately when he retired, the committee would not agree to this unless we gave up existing storage areas which we were not prepared to do.

By the early 1960s, I had purchased a number of antique clocks and was beginning to acquire quite a collection. I first became interested in these a little before 1950 when I found an oak-cased clock in a cottage at Great Tew. I obtained it in exchange for an arm chair! It was made by Jno. Paine who is recorded, by Dr Beeson in his book *Clockmaking in Oxfordshire 1400–1850*, as a maker at Hook Norton about 1840; it therefore had local interest. Early in 1950, I bought a longcase clock made by Geo. Clarke of Whitechapel from Wing Commander Hugh Patterson who was then living at Hitchin; this led to a lifelong friendship with him and his wife; I paid £52 for it – a good 8-day movement in a walnut case dating from about 1720. This was the beginning of my real interest in old clocks. I read some books and found many people who were prepared to help me. One of the first was Frank Young at Witney who gave me a lot of information and advice and let me have a copy of Britten's *Old Clocks and Watches and their Makers*; he also found me a copy of Baillie's *Watch and Clock Makers of the World*. Soon afterwards I bought, for £30, an ebonised bracket clock from Alex Podd at Dunstable; the repeat train was missing, the escapement had been converted and the hands were wrong but it was a good movement by C. Gould (not Christopher) in the original case *c.*1725.

In Oxford I found a small lantern clock by G. Langford which was thrown in as makeweight when I bought a bachelor's chest. Hugh Patterson let me have a small timepiece by McCabe for £22, he also sold me an ebonised bracket clock by Robert Seigneur for £62; the movement of this had suffered very badly and I eventually

A longcase clock in walnut by George Clarke of Whitechapel.

An ebonised bracket clock by Charles Gould.

Above: A small lantern clock by George Langford c. 1749.
Right: An ebonised bracket clock by Robert Seignoir (1645 - 1686). During Barry's lifetime, this was the only known example with a chapter ring signature c. 1683.

gave it up in despair. At length, I sold it for about what it had cost me. Some years later I saw this same clock illustrated as the only known example of this maker with a chapter ring signature, dating from *c*.1688 – it had been completely restored.

In the fifties, I obtained a turret clock movement made by Stockford of Thame; this came from Ewelme Church and was the subject of much correspondence with Dr Beeson. I saw him frequently and visited him at Adderbury when he was preparing his books. I managed to get the clock going and sold it to Edwards of Basingstoke. Around the same time I bought the movement, which had been discarded, from the clock in Witney Church; this was a very heavy, large, chiming piece of machinery made, I think, by Gillet & Johnson about 1850/75. It was not really very interesting but Hugh Patterson sent some RAF transport to collect it with the idea of erecting it at Henlow where he was stationed.

All this was before I met Godfrey Hands who came to live in Burford in 1963. He had a number of good clocks himself and opened the door for me to enter the real collecting world; through him I came to know a great many other clock collectors and members of the Horological Society. Our mutual interests took us around the country and to London; I made many friends and had access to many homes. The high prices that have now become accepted as values were unthought of and we derived much enjoyment in meeting and examining each other's prized possessions. I have memories of a large gathering at New Hayward – of having supper in Tim Horwood's farm kitchen – of visiting Kenneth Ullyatt at Glycine House and also at Hampton and buying a unique olivewood table clock from Dick Benford's collection; this was thought to be the only one by William Knottesford in existence. Later I was offered the almost identical twin which, foolishly, I did not buy.

We journeyed many miles and had many adventures with clocks. There was an expedition to Hove with Tim Horwood and Godfrey Hands where we found a Knibb bracket; it had been re-cased but we could find nothing wrong with the movement and I bought it for £1,100. It might be said that many of our travels were unfruitful but to me they were enjoyable and added to my knowledge and experience. Even in those days, the market was well combed and many doubtful specimens were offered. However, thanks to the guidance of those who knew much more than I did, I avoided many of the pitfalls; I cannot remember buying anything which deceived me, although with my eyes open, I bought many that were not 'quite right'.

The majority of clocks in my collection were acquired from personal friends and acquaintances on a basis of mutual trust but no one can travel far in the collecting world without becoming involved with dealers and I have known a great many. Most were genuine and honest, some knew very little about clocks and some needed to be approached with caution. All of them, understandably, were looking for profit. A number were collectors themselves and, on the whole, I got on well with most of them. I knew Meyrick Neilson very well when he was stationed in Yorkshire; he was then a brigadier in the regular army and he used to call in to see me on his way to Tetbury. When he retired he went to live there and started to trade in clocks. He became very well known internationally in a class of clocks (and prices) far above my standard. I developed many contacts including Geoffrey Bell of Winchester, Oliver Bentley of Leicester, R. C. Hart of Chiddingford who sold me a McCabe, No. 916, which became famous and Charles Allix who viewed my collection when he was writing his book on carriage clocks.

A table clock by William Knottesford, in an olive wood case with ebony columns c. 1675.

Clock (No. 916) made by James McCabe (Royal Exchange), Gothic style with brass inside case.

The inside of the McCabe clock seen on the previous page.

An ebonised, longcase clock by Thomas Tompion numbered 540 on both the movement and case.

As my collection grew, I weeded out, sold or exchanged those of lesser importance but I never paid unrealistic prices for any. Owing to fortuitous circumstances, there is no doubt that items in my collection reached considerable value but they did not represent a very large outlay and over the years I have derived a great deal of enjoyment from them. One in my collection, a clock by John Elliott, was later advertised in 1972 by Aspreys in *Country Life* as an 'outstanding clock' and at one time I owned two clocks by Thomas Tompion. Many of the clocks passed through my hands as the result of amicable dealings with friends and acquaintances; Godfrey Hands and I, on many occasions, passed clocks to and from one another in the form of sales and exchanges – all on the most friendly of terms and at reasonable prices. About 1971 I acquired a rare clock by Henry Jones, which I was offered by Aspreys; this was in a walnut case and had Dutch striking and was quite reasonable. I cannot say the same however about the last clock that I purchased to add to my collection. This was an Edward East timepiece in an olivewood case the total cost of which came to £2,500. In view of current high values, it seems unlikely that I shall add any more to the collection that I have gathered together.

In about 1964 I had dealings with B.C. Pickard who lived at Dorchester in Dorset, from him I bought several good hammered gold coins which have become one of my best investments. The acquisition of these, together with the clocks that I had retained, provided a very sound, appreciating asset at a time when money was rapidly losing its value.

It had reached a point of no return

I had reached a point at which I had much more money than I needed. I was no longer particularly concerned as to what I received from the profits that the business was making; although this was doing well, I took only a small proportion of the totals that were distributed. The other directors were receiving generous amounts which should perhaps have been ploughed back into the firm as capital and not distributed so freely. However, at the time, it was only viewed in the light of tax saving and it was, no doubt, confidently assumed that the scale of profit would continue. In 1962 the distributable profit was over £21,000, in 1963 over £26,000, in 1964 £27,000, and in 1965 over £30,000 by which year the turnover had reached £613,000.

In 1965 the affairs of all the companies continued to flourish but Cousins was becoming concerned about the economics of Bartlett Brothers Industrial Ltd and Bartlett Brothers 1960 Ltd doing the same type of work and trading as separate entities. We had many discussions about this and I think we all had in our minds the consultants' report (prepared in 1962), together with their recommendations. I am not sure how much Day and Driver were influenced by the findings, but at the end of 1964 they had decided that they could work together both amicably and efficiently. As a result, it was agreed that they should be given equal status as joint managing directors. Bartlett Brothers Industrial Ltd purchased all the shares in the other companies and the name was later changed to Bartlett Brothers (Witney) Ltd.

Cousins and I welcomed the new arrangements and to some extent relaxed; I think we felt that we had done all we could to provide the opportunity for success. The responsibility was now squarely in the hands of Day, Driver, Dingle and those who were actively engaged in the running of the business. I myself, as well as Cousins and to some extent John Welch, had derived considerable capital benefit when the original Bartlett Brothers Ltd was liquidated in 1960. The sale of the shares of Bartlett Brothers (1960) Ltd and Bartlett's Joinery Ltd provided us with more. Mary, however, owned nearly all

Front row, left to right: C. Day, E. Bartlett Taylor, A. J. Timms, J. Cousins, C. Driver. Back row, left to right: Jim Barker, C. Aucutt, F. Buckingham, J. Dingle, Bob Hinksman, and C. French

the shares in Rolyat and benefited to the greatest extent. This plant company had been under my personal control since its inception in 1951. It had thrived. We had provided all the mechanical plant for the needs of the other companies at rates considerably lower than normal charges and had made a profit. We employed two drivers, two mechanics and a clerk and by ploughing back most of the profit by 1965 we owned over £20,000 worth of plant. This was written down to £8,000 and we had a reserve in the bank of about £4,000; all of which was handed to the new company for £12,500.

Bartlett Brothers (Witney) Ltd started trading as a consolidated company, owning all the shares of the other companies, on 13th March 1965. We were all full of enthusiasm and optimism for the future. The whole of 75 High Street was taken over as offices so that all the staff were working under the same roof; Howe was accommodated on the ground floor of No. 77. The area of the joiners' shop was increased to almost double its original size and the yard was reorganised. The years of 1966, 1967 and 1968 were years of expansion; by 1968 the turnover for the year had risen to over a million but profits had not kept pace with increased turnover.

After Cousins remarried, he enjoyed travelling and was often abroad for short periods but we had frequent consultations and were never out of touch for very long. In June 1968, shortly after he returned from a trip to New York, he died after a short illness. In

him we lost the architect and driving force which had contributed so much to all the progress that had been achieved since those days in the early 1930s when we started working together. I am proud to have been associated with him in what had become a large company and we had both been able to look back with some satisfaction on the results of our efforts.

In the difficult times that lay ahead I greatly missed him; we had worked together for nearly fifty years and looked at things in much the same way. The consultations we had had over major problems were part of my life and we seldom disagreed. Administration had been almost entirely in his hands, he had worked more closely with the staff, understood their problems and they seemed willing to take his advice; he had been able to lead them much better than I could. Without him I had to make decisions which affected the whole future of the company in consultation with much younger directors whose views and outlook sometimes differed greatly from my own. I did not really disapprove of their major policies but I could not bring myself to enjoy or even approve of some of the methods of building that had been adopted. I was prepared to accept however that in the fierce competition that prevailed some of their methods were the only way by which we could survive. I hoped that we should still be able to maintain the standards of integrity, respect and service that we had tried so hard to achieve.

We were still pinning our faith on increased turnover and things were made worse by further expenditure in 1969. The office accommodation was improved and extended for additional staff and the area of the joiners' shop was increased. By this year turnover had risen to well over a million pounds. Looking back with hindsight it is not difficult to see the mistakes that were made. In the first place we fell into the trap of looking on increased turnover as a remedy for falling profits. Although I was never in favour of so much expansion, I did little to dissuade the others and to be fair, I took some pride in seeing the business expand. Lack of capital obviously had a bearing on our difficulties and in the latter stages it became acute. In the early thirties we were in a similar position, then we had almost no capital but we knew how to cut down on costs and we recovered with the help and support of our employees.

At the end of 1969 the company lost several loyal staff and conditions were changing fast; I had spent my active years with many of these people and those who took their places were almost unknown to me; sub-contractors and piece workers were taking over from direct labour and labour costs were becoming of paramount importance. Some of the older staff found it difficult to fit into the pattern of a larger organisation and amongst these was Frank Buckingham. He had been an excellent foreman and site organiser particularly on work carried out for Smiths of England. With reorganisation of the companies, he became involved in administration and other duties. He had started as an apprentice in 1928 and I had been concerned with him for a large slice of his life. I understood his position and had myself spent much of my life on sites; I tended to avoid being involved with administration and left it very much to Cousins. My grandfather, Joseph, had I believe, a similar outlook and was much happier away from the office. Rather than leave the company, Frank took over the organisation of a scheme at Benson and I believe felt far happier being directly involved on a project. Cousins and I had known exactly what was going on everywhere and we had kept a tight hold on what others did and how they did it. I am convinced that, where it is possible, 'the mud on the farmers' boots is the best manure'.

At the peak of the credit squeeze, at the time of the Rolls Royce crash, it was difficult to raise money anywhere and in the early part of 1971, I began to have serious doubts about the ability of the company to survive and retain its independence. Around this time I was able to discuss the problem with John Welch who has been in the background of all my business life ever since he first started to practise in Witney – when we were both very young. He has been my friend, my solicitor and my advisor and has always been ready with help and advice without stint or thought of personal gain. At this difficult time I also sought the help of my friend Godfrey Hands who had managed several large branches of the Midland Bank in London before his retirement; he obviously had considerable experience of company finances. After some negotiation, a loan was arranged with Lloyds Bank.

After Cousins died, I have great admiration for what was achieved by Day, Driver and Dingle. It was not always possible to get them to see things from my viewpoint – it may be that they were right and I was wrong. Each generation is so sure that it is doing things the right way! Most of the responsibilities of the day-to-day running of the business fell on their shoulders and I am grateful for their loyalty and their unstinted efforts which accomplished much, but the ultimate responsibility lay on my shoulders and I was growing old.

I found I could not cope with problems and difficulties in the way

Year	Turnover
1928	profit nill
1929	profit nill
Business transferred	to Ernest Bartlett Taylor
1932	£ 7,261
1933	£ 12,000
1934	£ 15,000
1936	£ 19,000
1938	£ 29,000
1939/40 ?	£ 40,000
1941	£ 41,000
War years	per year c. £ 32,500
1945	£ 30,000
1946	£ 32,000
1947	£ 50,000
1948	£ 65,000
1950	£ 70,000
1953	£125,000
1956	£200,000
1958	£381,000
1963 as company group	well over £500,000
1965	£613,000
1969	well over £1,000,000

Annual turnover for Bartlett Brothers, 1932 to 1969

that I once did and I tended to step aside and let others deal with them. I had lost the ability to see things through and I had lost my enthusiasm for progress; sometimes I felt very tired. Really all the anxieties of running the business seemed pointless. I did not need any income from it and there was no one in the family to continue it. It had reached a point of no return because it had grown so much as to become unmanageable in the form in which we had started it; all the anxieties and effort to keep it going were only for the benefit of those whose wages we paid. I was increasingly concerned that we might reach a state of insolvency. Not only would the stigma of this be painful to me and those directly concerned, but I worried also about those employees who had worked with me for so long; we were fighting a losing battle against competitive tendering and a spiral of inflationary costs. All this was in my mind when in 1973 the possibility of an amalgamation was mooted, but the credit for any preliminary negotiations must lie with Day and Driver. When details of a possible take-over by Elmers of Long Crendon were put before me, I had no hesitation in agreeing to an exploratory discussion with them. It seemed the obvious way out of a situation that had become untenable. The business would continue and no-one need lose their

BARTLETT BROTHERS (WITNEY) LTD

Quality Builders Since 1852

REGISTERED OFFICE
75 HIGH STREET
WITNEY, OXON OX8 6LX
TELEPHONE: WITNEY 3484-8

YOUR REF.

OUR REF.

Holding Company:	Directors:
DAVID C. ELMER LTD	D. C. ELMER Chairman
REGISTERED IN	P. P. BOYLES ⎫ Joint Managing
ENGLAND	F. A. BUTT ⎭
NO.	A. GARDNER, C.A. Secretary
757970	M. W. ELMER

REGISTERED OFFICE:
High Street · Witney · OX8 6LX   TELEPHONE: 0868 3484

FROM THE GROUP MANAGEMENT OFFICE

Headed paper after the merger of Bartlett Brothers with Elmers.

employment. No-one need suffer financially. The use of the premises would continue and I would receive a rent. I am certain that the decision to hand over the business to Elmers was the right one and taken at the right time – it seemed almost a miracle!

I cannot say I have no regrets. I had been personally involved in the affairs of the business for over fifty years. It was sad to see it leave the control of any member of the Bartlett family after over 120 years. I felt a sense of relief to have the burden that I had carried entirely alone for eight years after Cousins died, lifted at last.

In general, it appeared that most people who took any interest in the company approved of the transfer to Elmers; most of the employees realised that their jobs were secure and I think most people understood that it was the best I could do. One person who disapproved was Uncle Oswald. I can understand his feelings because all his life the business had been in the family and he was nearing one hundred years of age. He had been very proud to see it prosper in its latter years, in fact, he often told me how proud his father and uncle would have been to see its prosperity. He did not realise how difficult the last years had been and ironically, in 1920, he had been the one person who tried to dissuade me from becoming involved in what he thought was a business without any future.

The arrangements that I was able to make with Elmers gave me a great many personal advantages; I still owned all the freeholds and the rent I received was reasonable and subject to frequent review. I had a free run of all the premises that were leased and I retained my own office. My association with those who controlled the firm was pleasant and amiable; I think we were mutually helpful to one another. I was able to keep in contact with the staff in the offices and the yard without becoming involved in the conduct of the business. I was able to do and go where I pleased. I have a lot to be thankful for.

Oswald and Jack Bartlett.

When I set out to provide some sort of picture of the impressions and feelings I have experienced during the small span of time I have been permitted to call my life, I did so in the hope that some of what I have written might prove of interest to later generations; I have found interest and enjoyment in acquiring details concerning the lives and habits of those who have lived in earlier times. Now, in the natural order of life, I cannot look forward to many more years on this earth and the time has come to bring to a close what I have set out to record. The process, which commenced as an amusement, has provided me with much comfort and occupation. I have been blessed with worldly things far beyond my deserts. I claim no credit for whatever has been achieved but I have no inclination to hold a post-mortem on my shortcomings which are legion. Although we are set on a course, we have free choice and free will in all our thoughts and actions, but I also feel that we are subject to a guiding hand which directs us – if we are prepared to be directed.

Few of the important events in my life (or what I look on as important events) have been the result of conscious effort on my part; effort does not always lead to the results we envisage. We can sometimes look back on events and recognise what seems to be a providential pattern. I have regrets, of course I have many regrets, I have doubts, doubts that I cannot answer and I have misgivings about the future of civilisation as we know it. I sometimes wonder if I should be thankful that I have no-one of my own flesh and blood to follow me, rather than dwell on what might have been.

I feel that there is little likelihood of the return of the conditions of life that I have experienced during my term here and I look back with profound gratitude on the memories of the civilisation I have known, memories of honourable labour …. of parents, relations and friends who gave me love …. the love of animals …. the pleasures of work and ambition …. good food and sufficient money and the contentment of a satisfying life. I feel regret that I have neglected to use more endeavour to alleviate the lot of those who have been denied health and happiness who may feel a sense of injustice and frustration that they have not been able to enjoy those things in life that there are to enjoy.

Those who are now young and those who follow will enter a new world. They will have the free choice and the free will to shape their lives and to accept or reject the guidance that is offered to them – for them the world gone by will be only a story told by those who lived it.

I would like to acknowledge all the help and cooperation that I have received from the family and others, particularly those who gave me so much support and advice in my very early days of inexperience. I wish to record my grateful thanks to them all and particularly those mentioned below:

Oswald Alfred Bartlett (Uncle Oswald) – for his influence and early training.

Joseph Francis Bartlett (Uncle Joe) – for his wisdom, advice and restraint.

James Edgar Cousins (Jim Cousins) – for his support, encouragement and wisdom.

John William Welch (John Welch) – for his advice and unstinted help.

Herbert William Ingram (Bill Ingram) – for his business and accounts advice.

Howard William Meredith (Howard Meredith) – for his help with materials during the war.

And finally, the most important influence on my life:

Mary Elizabeth Taylor (my wife) – whose unfailing judgement guided our affairs. Whose care, organisation and management enabled things to run so smoothly at home. Who supported me in all that I undertook. Who celebrated our successes, shared our difficulties and defeats and gave so much of herself so unselfishly.

A rather cruel enlargement of the only known view of Barry and Mary Taylor in later life.

THE EPILOGUE

By the Reverend John Henry Cook
(22nd June 1911 - 10th December 2011)

For some years prior to 1968 Witney Parochial Church Council had employed Bartletts, the leading local builders, to cope with the upkeep and repairs of the four Church buildings, St. Mary's, Holy Trinity, St. John the Baptist at Curbridge and St. Luke's. The managers of the two Church schools, St. Mary's School on Church Green and the Batt School in the town centre, had also employed Bartletts for the same purposes. The Rectory and Assistant Clergy houses were also customers. When Bartletts ceased trading Mr Rymills, the architect and surveyor living on Church Green, advised to transfer custom to Messrs Fisher and Townsend.

During the time of reliance on Bartletts, the head of the firm was a regular worshipper at the Parish Church and at the same time a very generous contributor to Church and School funds; so much of his giving was done anonymously and it is true to say that I never knew the amounts of his giving and did not probe to find out. When I became the Rector of Witney in 1968, the leading churchwarden was wise and kind enough to tell me about Barry Taylor's generosity, warning me not to ask for financial support because Barry Taylor would always respond to general appeals by bringing large cheques to the Rectory; invariably such gifts were to be anonymous. After my retirement in 1978, my successor disregarded this advice (which I had conscientiously passed on to him) and made a purpose visit to Barry Taylor to raise money for some project. True to form Barry rejected his request and the rejection was followed by Barry transferring his Church attachment to Swinbrook! I, in my retirement, never discussed the occurrence, but our own personal relationship continued until he died.

In my early days in Witney, Barry was a great and practical supporter as I struggled against the Church authorities who strove to force me to accept accommodation in the old mansion near the west end of St. Mary's Church with its large unwieldy rooms and cellars, 3½ acres of garden with stabling and groom's living quarters! The Bishop of Reading, Bishop Knell, became a supporter of my cause and finally the Bishop of Oxford, Harry Carpenter, and his wife Urith came to inspect the situation. He called on the Church Commissioners to send a deputation of three architects and surveyors, all of whom gave support to my endeavour to avoid living in the old rectory building (now known as Trelawney House). The property was bought by the County Education Department who required additional accommodation for the Witney Grammar School which was to become a comprehensive school. A small portion of the old rectory garden was retained for the possible provision of a new rectory; that land has not been used yet and is treated as glebe. Suffice it to record that Barry supported me, as did the Church members at St. Mary's, in my persistent refusal to accept the old building and subsequently whilst I secured 22 Church Green, an ideal building for a rectory. Such support was offered without any criticism and to have Barry's endorsement was both valuable and much appreciated.

Barry Taylor never sought publicity but he offered good fellowship to a chosen few, rich or poor alike, and when he knew of hardship, he always responded with practical sympathy. While I was Rector, he took a leading part in transcribing the registers of Witney Parish - indeed a labour of love which he enjoyed as he delved amongst the records of the past and the experiences which former parishioners had either enjoyed or endured.

His interest and practical involvement with the firm of Bartletts decreased with advancing years particularly after the death of his close colleague James (Jim) Cousins. Of course, I was not aware of the business side of Barry's life but when the time came for him to relinquish his place as head of the firm, he was concerned that the high standards expected of the organisation would be hard to maintain after the business was sold.

He replaced his former commitments with an increasing interest in the welfare of Witney Church affairs and his generosity led to his provision of a house in Woodstock Road for the resident assistant curate. Barry was fully in agreement when, in 1968, I was able to sell the house in Woodstock Road and with the proceeds acquire 9 Church View Road; this meant that the curate could be closer to local housing developments at Smith's Estate and Burwell Farm. The house at 9 Church View Road was occupied by two curates in succession, Revd's Warren and Perceval; later the residence of the curate was moved to what had been the headmaster's house at the Batt School in order to have an official Church presence there and to secure the welfare of the school buildings. The Church then used 9 Church View Road as a tenancy for local school teachers but this arrangement proved unsuccessful and it was decided that the property should be sold. After an independent valuation of £16,000 I was able to purchase the house to live in during my retirement and following this, Barry's original loan was be repaid to him.

My wife and I experienced a generous act of thoughtfulness when we were vacating the Rectory, our happy home on Church Green. The costs of the move and that reduction in our way of life were unavoidably putting pressure on our finances and Barry decided to offer us a temporary interest-free loan, repayable when we had re-established ourselves. We accepted the loan and after three years we paid back what he had loaned to us - nobody else knew of that thoughtful gesture which was so timely and which at the same time did not impinge on our own self-respect.

Barry wanted to use what was in his power to benefit others - he had a real understanding of stewardship and with that ideal he must have conceived the idea of setting up the charitable trust (The Bartlett Taylor Charitable Trust) which could continue to uphold and discharge what he had begun. It has always seemed to me that Barry had read Verse 15 of Chapter three in the Book of Ezekiel; Ezekiel was guided by God to bring succour to those captive exiles in Babylon. He didn't harangue these sad and impoverished people, telling them what they ought to be doing with what they had not got, but he wrote "Where they sat, I sat", putting himself alongside them, sharing and caring. Barry's latter years were much occupied in sharing and caring and his Charitable Trust continues where Barry left off – a wonderful legacy.

Barry was a frequent visitor at our home and our relationship developed so that Barry's loneliness, after the death of his wife, benefited as did that of the Cooks! It was the privilege and joy of my wife, Marjorie, and myself to offer and to accept hospitality from Barry, either in our home or at a favourite restaurant in Eynsham where he liked to have home cooking. Quite often, he would add to the lunch party and Theresa Smith, widow of Tom Smith who had owned a joinery works, would be included along with Mrs Barber who faithfully looked after Barry in his home, acting as housekeeper and who was regarded as a trusted friend. Whenever he visited us in Church View Road, he invariably brought a small bag of walnuts, gathered from the large tree in his garden.

For Barry, nothing was ever too small or too large, he gave what he had. Barry was a strange mixture of generosity and frugality; in his own home he believed in harsh economies, insisting on a way of life which included self-denial in order that he could dispense sympathy and practical support to others who were struggling with adversity. He had sampled hard times in and with his own family, especially after his father's death and couldn't stand by and see others reduced to hopelessness.

In due course Barry's health began to deteriorate, but his housekeeper, helped by various health carers, enabled Barry to die in his own home fortified by Holy Communion. It was my privilege to administer Private Holy Communion in his own home the night before he died, as I had done for his wife Mary when she died years previously. It was my privilege also to be able to conduct Barry's funeral service in St. Mary's Church, where he had worshipped for so long, because the Rector was absent in India.

Some readers may wonder whether my association with Barry was indeed a reality and factual. I was overjoyed recently (summer 2011) to have found endorsement of this in my personal Visitor's Book where the signatures of Mary, his wife, and his own were written in the first of my "Church parties for Church people" when we took up residence at the new Rectory at 22 Church Green.

The Reverend John Cook 2011

In his Christmas card to my family, which was received a few days after his death, the Reverend Cook wrote:

'I thank you for letting me take a small part in recording the life and times of Barry T – a faithful friend of mine'.

In fact the Reverend Cook proved to be inspirational. When it seemed that Barry's story might remain concealed in a number of cardboard boxes, it was he that gave me the encouragement to go ahead. Over several years we shared the stories, explored family connections and photographs and at length and with his blessing, the project was started in earnest in 2011.

Rosemary Warner

GLOSSARY

Bee skep - an early bee hive made out of braided or twisted straw coiled to form a conical shape.

Brattice felt - a coarse felt treated with tar.

Bressummer beam - a horizontal load-bearing beam often with masonry above.

Delta metal - an alloy of copper, zinc and ferro-manganese.

Fire dogs - a device to raise logs above the hearth to improve air circulation.

Lead cames - lead bars used to hold the glass in the construction of leaded windows.

Leat stream - an open water-course conducting water to a mill.

Pargeting a chimney - rendering the inside of a chimney using 'fat' mortar - mortar without sand or cement but to which cow dung is added.

Peck and shovel - the peck was a less cumbersome and more easily transported implement than the larger pick axe, but served a similar purpose.

Pit dogs - a G-shaped device for anchoring heavy timber before sawing.

Pit saw - a long two-handled (two-man) saw for cutting heavy timber.

Quetta bonded brick work - a method used to produce strengthened, load bearing brickwork for industrial use. The first courses of bricks would be laid on wet concrete and voids constructed within the brickwork itself, into these steel rods would be placed. The voids would then be filled with concrete.

Rent laths -roughly sawn strips of wood.

Riparian rights - river-bank rights associated with ownership.

Roof hip - a sloping edge of roof, an alternative to a gable end.

Swept roof valleys - a highly skilled process whereby wedge-shaped slates are arranged on areas where two roof surfaces meet.

Rope blocks - parts of a pulley assembly through which the ropes were threaded.

Slaking lime - leaving the lime in a container to heat up naturally.

Spit jack - a mechanism for holding and rotating meat over an open fire.

Straw band twister - an implement to hold and twist straw into a rope.

Torched with hair mortar - spaces filled with mortar reinforced with animal hair.

The world gone by. We began with the frontispiece looking into a prosperous and thriving yard. To finish we have a similar view looking into the derelict yard. Take a walk through the gateway today, above which it still proudly proclaims 'Bartlett Builder', and you will see a different world again. The buildings to the left still stand, now occupied by the Witney & District Museum.